MW00679123

CREATIVE GARDEN DESIGN: PATTERNS

CREATIVE GARDEN DESIGN: PATTERNS

INSPIRING IDEAS FOR CREATING MOOD, PROPORTION, AND SCALE FOR EVERY LANDSCAPE

JACK WALLINGTON

Krause Publications
An imprint of Penguin Random House LLC
penguinrandomhouse.com

Copyright © UniPress Books Ltd 2020

Published by arrangement with
UniPress Books Ltd.
All rights reserved. No part of this book
may be reproduced, transmitted or stored
in an information retrieval system in any
form or by any means, graphic, electronic
or mechanical, including photocopying,
taping and recording, without prior
written permission from the publisher.

Penguin supports copyright. Copyright
fuels creativity, encourages diverse voices,
promotes free speech, and creates a vibrant
culture. Thank you for buying an authorized
edition of this book and for complying with
copyright laws by not reproducing, scanning,
or distributing any part of it in any form
without permission. You are supporting
writers and allowing Penguin to continue
to publish books for every reader.

Printed in China
1 3 5 7 9 10 8 6 4 2

ISBN 978-1-44035-511-0

Conceived, designed and produced by
UniPress Books Limited

Edited by John Andrews
Proofread by Jane Roe
Index by Marie Lorimer
Designed by Fogdog.co.uk

Contents

Introduction
What is pattern?

When you look at a garden, you may feel drawn to plants whose colours and shapes have been arranged in a particular way. A row of three repeated pots containing the same plants might catch your eye more than any other feature. Simple patterns, with their sense of order or neatness, draw attention and look satisfying—but why?

We all recognize pattern, but what exactly is it? On a basic level, a pattern is the rhythm and repetition of shape, line, or color—and, indeed, sound and touch—often, but not always, equally spaced. Pattern needs only to draw on one of these elements—for instance, entirely different shapes spaced equally, or a series of circles with spacing that doubles with each new circle. Some large-scale patterns might contain many smaller patterns, which can create something so complex that the individual patterns are only spotted when examined more closely. Then there's abstract pattern, where repetition and equal spacing or size are thrown out the window. Instead, the common thread is a regularity in style or theme, such as color.

IMPACT AND LOGIC

Essentially, a pattern, as opposed to a scene in a painting or photo, occurs when shapes or objects are positioned so they relate to one another, linked by repetition, rhythm, size, color, spacing, a matching style or combinations of any of these things. There's a regularity between them. Such a pattern may grab attention, like the feathers on a peacock, or it may merge into its surroundings, such as a zebra's stripes, which help the animal to blend in with its habitat. Understanding why and how pattern can have varying degrees of impact on a garden is often overlooked, but it's as important as, say, color or texture— sometimes even more so when pattern is used as the underlying framework unifying all other elements.

Any shape can be used to create pattern, from simple geometric or curvilinear outlines to incredibly detailed images of nature, people, animals, and other objects. Pattern is often pictured in two dimensions, but, as you'll see throughout this book, it appears in three dimensions as well, and nowhere more so than in gardens.

By opening our eyes to pattern, we find the entire natural world—in fact, the universe—consists of patterns and, in understanding their logic, we can make better sense of the space around us. Whether it's the repeated shape of the leaves on a tree, the petals on a flower, honeycomb in a beehive, the prints on our fingers or a flock of geese in flight, pattern has a greater impact on our lives than we often realize.

Patterns and people

One glance at the houseplants—cacti, succulents, and the like—in anyone's home and you'll notice that, however subconsciously, they have been chosen for their strong pattern. Something within human beings is unintentionally drawn to their shape and form.

Animals are programed to recognize and read pattern and sometimes even make it. Pattern is ingrained in the human psyche, too. Not only do we admire patterns and love to create them, but we're also particularly adept at doing so.

For humans, pattern is hardwired into our DNA—a hugely complex material which itself forms the most remarkable patterns. Humans evolved using pattern recognition to survive. They learned to read the pattern of the seasons as the days shorten, the Earth's shadow on the moon changing through the month, the footprint trails of prey and the markings and leaf arrangements of particular plants that signaled whether they were edible or deadly—like the toxic red-capped fly agaric mushroom (right).

Words, sounds, computer code, even the text you are reading now, are all based on a complex series of patterns and our amazing ability to interpret them. We find these patterns comforting because they structure our world and help us to make sense of it. And we have also adapted to find pattern satisfying and attractive, reflected in the myriad patterns filling every high street fashion and homeware store.

PATTERN CREATORS

Humans have long created pattern. Prehistoric cave paintings, such as the mysterious hands (opposite, top right) dating back 10,000 years, found at the Cueva de las Manos (Cave of Hands) in Argentina, include patterns within them, for reasons we can only guess at. Over time this use of pattern evolved into the written word, art, design, and even eventually into secret coded communications during times of war.

The wide use of decorative patterns is closely linked to the Industrial Revolution, when the automation of human skills allowed mass production of patterned furnishings and clothes for the first time. The ability to create patterns on a huge and affordable scale boosted the popularity of wallpaper, fabric, and other designs from Victorian companies such as Morris & Co and Liberty. During this period, nature took center stage for most patterns, such as leaf shapes, flowers, and exotic animals, bringing the beauty of the wild into the home.

When we create pattern we tend to do so in a more precise way than in nature—straightening lines, ironing out imperfections, evening up sizes, smoothing shapes. Whether for ease of drawing or manufacture, or purely for esthetic reasons, this simplification of pattern has been a driving force in bringing order and

structure to our homes, gardens, and workplaces. Windows, walls, fences, staircases—everywhere is an opportunity for pattern, from elaborate to minimalistic.

FUTURE PATTERN

Today, pattern is as important and popular as ever. Clothes and furnishings with pattern continue to come in and out of fashion, while patterned wallpaper and tiles are still used as focal points. Although increasingly minimalist, architecture still features pattern, albeit with grand-scale components and an emphasis on geometric shape. At the same time, a modern trend in pattern has developed, particularly in gardens, that seeks to copy the free-flowing, less restrained patterns seen in nature. Minimalism and natural profusion may appear to be two contrasting styles, but they work together, showing the ever-evolving power of pattern.

Patterns in gardens

In gardens, pattern is everywhere—on leaves, in plant shapes, repeated in borders, fixed into patio paving and seat cushion fabrics. More complex patterns appear in plantings, where gardeners seek to create a tapestry of leaf texture, color repetition, and form that changes over time. Combined, all these elements can transform the way a garden looks and feels.

Pattern is almost always pivotal in making a design work, bringing logic and movement to a space. A pattern in planting or hard landscaping can give a garden instant visual impact as well as create structure and a relaxing flow, even helping to guide people through its spaces.

LESSONS FROM HISTORY

In Morocco, ancient Moorish gardens overflow with pattern from carvings, friezes, tiles, the garden layout itself, and the positions of plants. Surprisingly, this isn't as overwhelming as you might expect, but is instead calming and beautiful. The factors that influence the way the patterns look, such as color, shape and texture, help to blend the myriad patterns to create something cohesive.

From historic garden plans and paintings we also know that medieval gardens contained pattern, in the surrounding architecture of loggias, arches, and trellis, as well as in their strict grid layouts. Parterres, in the later Renaissance period, particularly in Italy and France, were filled with patterned layouts marked with bedding and low hedging. Their unnatural structure and strictly imposed order exuded a sense of formality, aimed at impressing through a show of power and wealth. Renaissance gardens could look either stark or cluttered depending on the number of elements, and today we see them as the most formal of all gardens.

Not all historic gardens were so rigidly structured, and the pull between formal structure and mimicking the informality of nature in gardens is as old as time. In Japan and China, the Shinto and Buddhist religions emphasized the importance of calmness, peace, and respect for nature, the essence of which was recreated in relaxed and informal gardens. Though not truly naturalistic, they were certainly an attempt to capture and appreciate the spirit of the wild. Hidden at first, even the most naturalistic-looking human-created garden will have a pattern within it, whether it's the layout of key spaces—like patios—the positions of rocks and other objects, or the placement of plants.

PATTERN TO THE FORE

Today, a new wave of gardeners and designers seeks to break from the molds of past gardens—driven by the desire to create something different and armed with a wealth of increased knowledge and a wider selection of materials and plants. Pattern in gardens is being pushed to new limits and used in fresh ways, while building on what gardeners have achieved in the past (see the features "Abstract patterns," pages 54–5, and "Contemporary urban gardens," pages 194–5).

The tussle between naturalistic and unnatural (formal) gardens is—as it always has been—at the forefront of contemporary garden design, with a slight bias toward the naturalistic. However, with the majority of the world's population now living in cities and towns, urban gardens, with their strict limitations on space, are driving a new form of relaxed-cum-formal garden, making the most of bold pattern on paving and walls, while still using plants to impose some natural pattern.

In times when flexibility in the use of space becomes increasingly important, the very essence of pattern is being explored by experimental gardeners, designers, and landscapers. Never has pattern been so important as a way to hold everything in the garden together. When executed well, pattern in your garden will be both visually arresting and the key to making the most of your outdoor space.

1 PATTERN INFLUENCERS

When you stop to examine patterns, you'll notice they have various influencing elements. These influencers affect the look and feel of a pattern—making it calm or exciting, modern or traditional, brash or subtle. Use these influencers to turn the pattern dial to the exact combination you want.

Color

You don't have to use it to make a pattern, but color can both boost a design and create depth. Take, for example, a simple design of checkered black and white squares. Change every other black square to red, and the colors gain a new pattern, layered over the first.

In gardens, color is a key ingredient. It can make a space feel lively or relaxed, draw the eye with a bold, clashing flourish or hide unwanted features by using harmonious shades that blend into the background.

To understand colors, it's best to start by differentiating between those that complement each other and those that simply relate to each other. Complementing colors sit at opposite ends of the color spectrum. Yellow and purple (right) are good examples, which, when used together in a garden, combine well, creating a sharp, exciting contrast. Use too many complementing colors, though, and your multicolored dream garden will induce a migraine; while no contrast at all makes a garden appear flat.

Relating colors, such as red and purple, sit together on the color spectrum and blend well in a garden. Other examples of colors that relate to each other in this way include blue and purple, yellow and green, and red and orange.

Colors also come in different shades, tones, and tints, such as the range from soft pastel pink to bold hot pink. Lighter tints—the pastels—are calming and lighten a space, while darker shades feel luxurious and more intimate. Furthermore, colors can create different perceptions, from "cool and calming" blues and greens to "hot and energetic" reds and yellows.

Above all, don't be bound by the rules, but choose colors you like. Feel free to play around with color to find what works best for you.

COLOR EFFECTS

The balancing of color in combination with pattern is endlessly interesting and the essence of how all gardens are designed. Choose your own palette and dot the colors around the garden—from plants to furniture—in patterns that feel right to you. Opposite, above, a relaxing color scheme of related pastels—blue *Eryngium*, buff brown *Allium* seed heads, and terracotta *Achillea millefolium*—is enlivened by contrasting burgundy *Allium sphaerocephalon* and deep green *Cupressus sempervirens* "Totem Pole."

Limiting the color scheme can make a space feel calmer, allowing shape and shadow to come to the fore. Opposite, below, a curved raised bed and striped horizontal fence panels stand out in a relaxed garden with a restrained palette.

BALANCING COLOR

Left, the pastel purple of *Verbena bonariensis* combines well with the closely related blue of *Eucalyptus gunnii* foliage and light gravel. A sympathetic contrast is added by the white of chamomile and agapanthus alongside the deep magenta of *Geranium* "Ann Folkard."

SUBTLE SCHEMES

Below, Lithuanian designer Ula Maria has used a limited color palette of green, rust, and gray to create a cohesive and informal garden. Her scheme allows the white of the tiles to sing out as a beautifully patterned focal point.

HIGH CONTRAST

Upping the contrast with *Cornus sanguinea* "Winter Flame," white-barked birch trees, flowering heather, and golden dwarf conifers (top) make for a dazzling winter display. Above, British designer Sarah Eberle uses tiles with strong, bold color to make pattern the unmissable center of attention. Right, repeated yellow pots containing *Agave attenuata* draw the eye at Jardin Majorelle in Marrakesh.

Texture

It's said that a garden should work even when viewed with no color, and doing so brings out the importance of texture. Imagine your garden in black and white (or better still, take a photo and change it to black and white)—how many different patterns and textures can you see?

Texture—such as smooth, fluffy, or rough—is created in a garden by the surface or overall appearance of a plant or material. These textures not only feel different but also look different when subjected to the play of light and shadow.

When you introduce pattern to a garden, texture is important where color is used but even more so where it isn't. Simply using two materials of the same color in different textures, such as smooth slabs next to rougher bricks, can transform a patio.

The same is true of planting—for example, a fluffy grass next to a large-leaved shrub in a similar shade produces textural contrast, as does a selection of plants growing next to hard materials.

Textural contrast allows you to create pattern and interest without constantly adding color, which could become overwhelming. Different textures can be used in a similar way to color, to make something stand out, or to give a scene more interest. A tiled wall pattern could be made using tiles in two different colors; alternatively, tiles of the same color but with different textures can create the same pattern. In a garden full of pattern, toned-down textural patterns create breathing space. The tactile nature of textures also plays an essential part in sensory gardens, where people with poor sight, or no sight at all, can still enjoy the plants and surfaces.

The absence of texture can also be effective. The smooth surfaces of rendered walls, for example, create a visual break in more complex areas of a garden. Rendered columns, such as on a house or a loggia, provide a minimalist pause, while creating their own simple pattern through repetition.

TEXTURE AND PATTERN

The courtyards at Bahia Palace in Marrakesh, with their intricate tiled floors surrounded by carved friezes in muted wood (left), offer a key lesson in texture. Although the patterns in the wood carvings are particularly complex, their singular color doesn't compete with the surroundings, but blends into them. The finely carved pattern also creates texture on the wood surface, becoming clearer the more you focus on it. The textured surface helps the large, smooth banana plant leaves to stand out, too.

ROUGH WITH THE SMOOTH

Smooth surfaces, on walls, paving, and containers, can give structure and focus to a relaxed garden of mixed plantings (left). The soft-looking textures of the materials contrast with the light, airy textures of the plants.

PLANTS VS LANDSCAPING

If these pictures were viewed in black and white, their patterns would still be clear, thanks to the strong textural contrast. Left, a patterned geometric rendered wall makes a focal point as it breaks up the soft texture of the hedges. Above, a minimalist combination of decking, paving, and grass allows the curve of a wall to stand out. Right, a repeating shaggy grass pattern contrasts with columns of circular wood stacks to create a dramatic but balanced living wall.

Shape

Important though color and texture are to garden pattern, shape is arguably the most critical factor. From basic lines, squares, circles, and triangles, through to the most detailed plantings, shape is the fundamental building block of pattern.

There are infinite combinations of shape, forming the foundation of all patterns. A basic repeating pattern of circles on a wall, such as the rows of concrete portholes at the Swiss National Museum (opposite, center), will tend to look clean and modern. A more complex pattern, involving multiple curves and intricate details, as you might find around medieval church buildings or in a Victorian garden, leans toward the traditional and formal. That said, complex pattern can look modern and vice versa, depending on shapes and how they are deployed—there are no set rules.

Patios display the most obvious use of shape, thanks to the outline of the overall area and the materials used (see pages 100–3), such as lines of decking, grids of rectangular paving, herringbone brick, and crazy paving. It's the shape that dominates more than color and texture.

Planting by its very nature includes a multitude of shapes in the form of leaves, flowers, stems, and structure (see pages 30–47). Dotting plants around a garden, you can utilize their shapes to create patterns and effects through repetition and mass grouping for sweeping design gestures.

Shape, more than any other feature, is everywhere, from walls to printed and painted materials, cushions to tiles, sculpture to furniture, and paths to pools. All are designed with shape at their heart, adding solid structure to gardens and forming a variety of patterns throughout a space.

LAYOUT AND STRUCTURE

A clean, sweeping lawn edge at Fairlight End, in Kent, UK (right), produces a striking shape that creates a strong structure, holding the entire garden together. A subdued color palette, dominated by greens, is enhanced with further shape from background topiary and a mass planting of upright *Pinus mugo* along the lawn edge.

STRIKING FOCAL POINTS

Above left, a round pool grabs the attention. Above right, rectilinear shapes are accentuated with solid weathered steel edges, a monolithic steel screen, and plants with shapely outlines. The consistent use of rectangles creates a sense of unity through shape. Left, a row of portholes uses obvious shape for a basic but eye-catching pattern.

FORM AND FOLIAGE

A simple square patio of brick (right) frames a jungle garden, where plant form and foliage take center stage. The shapes of the palm fronds and trunks dominate the scene.

Perspective

Pattern and perspective in gardens are intertwined. Pattern can be used to alter perspective—manipulating how space is perceived—or it can direct where you gaze or walk. Equally, a pattern's look will change as your viewpoint changes.

An avenue of trees forms a basic repetition pattern, which, viewed as an entire row (right), makes a strong focal point. Yet, if rows of trees are viewed from one end (below), the pattern enhances your perspective, as the eye is drawn along the avenue, directing where you go. Edges of paths and decking laid in the same direction as the angle of an adjoining path or door do the same, the lines leading you to the next area.

We rely on pattern to tell us how the world works. If lines of perspective are distorted, the eye is fooled into seeing an enhanced view of that world. Areas in

a garden can be made to feel larger or deeper than they actually are by incorporating the subtle use of such optical illusion in pattern design.

Classic examples of pattern used to distort garden perspective include laying slabs or decking horizontally to make a space feel wider, or laying them lengthways for a greater sense of depth. Narrowing a lawn slightly at the end furthest from a house, or making the furthest pots in a row of pots smaller than those at the front, produce features that appear longer than they really are. Vertical space can be exploited, too. Tall ornamental grasses, for example, can make narrow planting areas feel bigger.

Other tricks include hidden garden boundaries and paths that wind out of sight. Removing perspective anchors in this way creates intrigue and the sense that there's more beyond what the eye can see.

PERSPECTIVE PLAY

In a formal garden at Plas Cadnant, in Wales (above), the eye is directed by the lines of the path and repeated topiary in a simple pattern that reinforces the view along a central perspective. The pattern draws your gaze to the pool, impelling you to walk toward it.

ENHANCING SPACE

Decking, with its long wooden stripes, is a useful tool for creating a greater sense of width and length in small areas. A tight space between buildings will feel wider if planks, or other linear flooring, run perpendicular across the narrowest distance (above). Balconies can be made to appear deeper or wider using the same trick.

Scale, balance, and proportion

The relative size of spaces, plants, and objects in a garden ultimately decides whether a garden design "feels" right or out of balance. And pattern plays a key part in this; too small and it can get lost, too big and it will dominate.

Scale and proportion are closely linked. Scale is how we measure one object against another to judge relative sizes. Proportion concerns how all those objects relate to each other as a whole. In a garden, most areas need to be at a scale that works for the people who will use them. A tiny pond next to a large house, for example, will feel out of proportion, as will a small cottage with a huge patio.

Balance is achieved when the scale of elements within a garden is in proportion and working in unison. If garden elements aren't well proportioned, the space will be unbalanced. Think of it in terms of visual weight. Put a bulky shed in a pocket-sized garden and it becomes the center of attention, tipping the balance too far in the wrong direction.

Pattern plays an important part in getting the balance right. The size of an area that's patterned, such as a patio, should be in proportion to everything else in the garden. The pattern itself should also relate seamlessly to the space. A highly detailed pattern could feel lost in a large area but easily visible in a smaller one.

That said, spaces in compact gardens often feel more balanced—and sharper—if they are made up of a limited number of large items, and even large-scale patterns. The alternative is to have lots of smaller items and plants, which can feel messy and cluttered.

Contemporary architecture and design favour less fussy hard landscaping, such as the use of a single material for a patio or wall. These large but simple areas help to make sense of more intricate, less structured features, such as meadows and naturalistic planting. Often the hard landscaping and planting areas are of a similar size, balanced by the textural differences between the two.

BALANCE

This compact urban garden feels perfectly balanced because the chunky sculptural planting, slabs, and chair are all roughly the same size; nothing dominates. The large, grid-like paving pattern and luxuriant architectural plants create a spacious feel.

PROPORTION

An enormous glass wall provides the cue for a pond created at the same width (top left). Both feel in scale with each other, well proportioned and balanced. On the other hand, get the proportions wrong and balance is lost, as is shown center left by the clash of scales between a tiny pond and a huge lawn.

SCALE

Substantial patterned stairs built at the same scale as fronds of *Dicksonia antarctica* tree ferns allow a small garden (right) to make the most of its limited space. The area feels balanced because both plant and material elements are large, which also ensures the pattern is clearly visible from a distance.

Framing and edging

Frames and edges enhance garden areas, particularly those with pattern. Frames give context to a view, or focus the gaze by blocking other views. Edges act like the frame of a picture, holding together pattern elements such as planting.

The most obvious frames are created by the windows and doorways you look through when viewing a garden from inside a building. Stepping into a garden, you can use the principle of the window to discover new framing opportunities, such as blocking views with shrubs and trees, or structures like sheds, arches, and pergolas. On a larger scale, walls and fences create a frame around a garden, too, indicating where the garden ends, while adding structural line and backdrop for planting and furniture.

The framing of a garden pattern, such as a view of a tiled wall or floor, can reinforce it as a focal point, directing your gaze to it and creating intrigue by concealing certain parts. Edges tell you where a patterned area begins and ends, and their clean, uncomplicated lines mark the transition from one garden feature into another. A row of bricks, for example, running around patio paving or smaller cobbles, can create an attractive progression between an area of hard material and a softer planting area.

Paths, patios, lawns, and planting beds all create natural edges, avoiding the need for a specific frame-like edge. Naturalistic plantings and meadows benefit particularly from a clean edge provided by an adjacent lawn or path, helping to make sense of their sometimes chaotic and complex patterns.

Knowing when not to use frames and edges is also important. A pattern with no edge can happily be painted onto a wall, or patterned tiles used only in the middle of a patio area. On top of that, a lack of framing always makes a space feel more open.

INTRIGUE AND FOCUS
Left, a gate arch frames the garden beyond, willing you to enter and discover what lies at the end of the path—and maybe around the corner. The arch also directs attention to the roughly symmetrical patterns in the planting, creating a simple frame around a living picture.

PATTERNED FRAMES

Frames can also act as carriers of pattern (left). Here, the patterned wooden arches match the bark of the trees and frame the busy planting around them.

GAINING THE EDGE

Edges to garden areas usually consist of stone, wood, or metal lengths that run along the ground. But there's nothing to stop you trying something more inventive, such as the well-spaced upright wooden posts below.

Unity

Unity is the combination of all principles discussed in this chapter and how they work together to make a garden feel as one, creating a unified space. As with so much in garden design, unity is subjective, but there are known ways of helping outdoor spaces to radiate cohesion.

Pattern can play a major role in unifying a garden or garden area. Patios and decking are primary features in most gardens, especially smaller urban gardens, and the choice of material and the pattern of laying are critical in unifying everything around them, as well as linking outdoor and indoor spaces. Such large pattern elements, which also include walls and fences, set the entire garden tone.

To assess unity—and introduce new patterns to enhance or maintain it—first look at your garden as a whole, as well as everything you can see beyond its boundaries. Consider using pattern in that wider context. Are there colors, textures, and shapes you can draw from neighboring buildings, trees, and landscapes? Does your building have existing shape or pattern on it already? Is the planting dominated by a certain color or shape? What is the layout?

By linking pattern to one or more of these existing elements in a garden, it will feel part of that place, rather than an alien addition. The pattern created by the form of a curved tree trunk, for example, can be mirrored in the shape of a winding path; the pattern of a patio can reflect something about a house, such as the shape of a particularly beautiful feature or the materials used in its walls.

Pattern doesn't have to be a direct match for a particular feature. The style of a garden should also be considered. A clean white carved patterned sculpture or a pattern on furniture may not be linked to anything in the garden, but tonally they may work with the hard landscaping and the overall contemporary style of the garden, making that the unifying factor.

CREATING HARMONY

A combination of woodland planting and patterned screen and paving in natural materials gives the garden on the left a sense of natural unity, enhanced by the color matching of chairs and flowers. Everything about the garden above, including its patterned hedges and unified materials, suggests relaxed formality.

BRINGING IT TOGETHER

Strong, well-proportioned shapes and soft earth tones make the garden above left feel warm and welcoming. A lesson in cohesion, the garden above right matches contemporary furniture with modern landscaping materials, all in the same neutral color palette. Although different shapes and textures, the various elements in the Zen garden on the right work perfectly together to create a real sense of calm.

BUSY GARDEN UNITY

British designer Chris Beardshaw shows, right, that gardens don't have to be minimalist to feel unified. Grays, gold, and copper are used for sculpture and paving, mirrored in the bark of the tree trunks and the silver of the *Cynara cardunculus* leaves. Color in the planting is repeated, forming a pattern of greens, purple, and white.

2

PLANTS WITH PATTERN

All plants have a pattern—in their stems, leaves, and flowers—but some are more striking than others. Use these selected superstars of the gardening world, with their clear, distinctive structure and visual drama, to command attention and instantly transform your garden through texture, shape, and flair.

NOTE: Each plant entry includes a hardiness rating, indicated by "H" and "Zone," based on the plant's preferred temperature. See the charts on page 219 for more information.

Leaf shape and texture
Trees

A tree always provides high impact—and a tree with a strongly patterned appearance even more so. The scale of a tree accentuates beautifully any regimented pattern as it spreads over a large surface area in the garden. Use trees as bold focal points or textured backdrops to other plants.

PITTOSPORUM TOBIRA

A shrub that eventually grows into a small tree. Its glossy, dark green leaves grow in uniform whorls, producing a satisfying repeated pattern across the plant. Scented yellow flowers appear in late spring.

↓ *Evergreen, 13 ft (4 m) tall, 8 ft (2.5 m) wide. Full sun to part shade. Soil moist, free draining. H3 / Zones 8–12*

DICKSONIA ANTARCTICA

Large fronds repeated around the top of the main trunk create a strong point of interest. The fronds themselves are detailed in a textured pattern.

↑ *Evergreen, 13 ft (4 m) tall, 13 ft (4 m) wide. Part shade to full shade. Soil moist, acid-neutral. H3 / Zones 9–12*

ACACIA PRAVISSIMA

Triangular phyllodes (enlarged leaf petioles with the leaf absent) form a repeated pattern along shoots and branches, firing off like fireworks in all directions. Perfect grown alongside plants with larger leaves. The shrub produces yellow flowers in spring.

→ *Evergreen, 13 ft (4 m) tall, 8 ft (2.5) m wide. Full sun. Soil free draining, acid-neutral. H3 / Zones 9–11*

SCIADOPITYS VERTICILLATA

A slow-growing tree with needles arranged like tufts at the end of branches. This feature creates a pattern across the tree from sapling to maturity.

← *Evergreen, 66 ft (20 m) tall, 39 ft (12 m) wide. Part sun. Soil fertile, slightly acidic. H6 / Zones 5–8*

PODOCARPUS HENKELII

A tree with narrow linear, drooping leaves arranged along branches so that the end of each branch carries a mop-shaped growth. These "mops" repeat across the tree, making a distinct pattern. See also *Podocarpus salignus*.

→ *Evergreen, 66–98 ft (20–30 m) tall, 66 ft (20 m) wide. Part shade to full sun. Soil moist loam or sandy. H3 / Zones 9–11*

TETRACENTRON SINENSE

Heart-shaped leaves hang alternately downward at equal intervals along spreading branches for a striking natural pattern. The tree displays strong red colors in fall and small yellow flowers in summer.

→ *Deciduous, 39 ft (12 m) tall, 26 ft (8 m) wide. Full sun to part shade. Soil fertile, well drained. H6 / Zones 6–7*

Leaf shape and texture
Shrubs

Shrubs have size but on a human scale. Their patterns grow from waist level to above head height, where you can see and touch them as they spread up from the ground. Grow patterned shrubs as centerpieces or among other plants, where they will both draw attention to other plants and act as a foil to them.

ARALIA ECHINOCAULIS
Thanks to its arrangement of opposite leaves on a highly geometric frame, this shrub offers one of the most structured patterns. Spikes run down its trunk and branches, creating a natural focal point.
↓ *Deciduous, 6½–19½ ft (2–6 m) tall. Full sun. Soil fertile, free draining. H6 / Zones 5–8*

ALOIAMPELOS STRIATULA
A bushy succulent that displays branches of chunky pointed leaves in repeated star shapes. In summer, yellow cone-shaped racemes of flowers appear vertically, producing yet more pattern.
→ *Evergreen, 8 ft (2.5 m) tall, 8 ft (2.5 m) wide. Full sun. Soil well drained. H3 / Zone 9*

EUPHORBIA MELLIFERA
A highly structured shrub with branches equally spaced from one another—a feature that becomes apparent when flower heads appear in early summer. The leaf pattern too makes the plant one of the best for pattern in the garden. See also *Euphorbia characias* subsp. *wulfenii.*
↑ *Evergreen, 8 ft (2.5 m) tall, 8 ft (2.5 m) wide. Full sun. Soil any well drained. H3 / Zones 9–11*

PINUS STROBUS "TINY KURLS"
The curling needles of this dwarf pine create a remarkable pattern, like a green head of curly hair. Needles are arranged in clumps that curl one way then the other, forming a complex matrix.
↑ *Evergreen, 6½ ft (2 m) tall, 10 ft (3 m) wide. Full sun. Soil damp, free draining. H7 / Zones 3–10*

VIBURNUM PLICATUM F. TOMENTOSUM "MARIESII"

Many viburnums have tiered branches, with flower heads held vertically, and none more so than "Mariesii." The shrub holds its flowers upright in spring, equally spaced on layered branches. See also *Viburnum plicatum* f. *tomentosum* "Kilimanjaro."

← *Deciduous, 13 ft (4 m) tall, 13 ft (4 m) wide. Full sun to part shade. Any soil. H6 / Zones 5–8*

SCHEFFLERA DELAVAYI

One of the hardy umbrella plants, with large compound palmate leaves that form a pattern similar to some rhododendrons, enhanced as the plant grows. See also *Schefflera taiwaniana*.

→ *Evergreen, 26 ft (8 m) tall, 26 ft (8 m) wide. Part sun to light shade. Soil fertile, well drained. H5 / Zones 7–8*

STACHYURUS CHINENSIS

For most of the year, *S. chinensis* is a pretty, if underwhelming, plant. But in late winter to early spring, yellow flower spikes point rigidly downward to form one of the most attention-grabbing displays of natural pattern in the garden.

← *Deciduous, 8 ft (2.5 m) tall, 13 ft (4 m) wide. Sun to part shade, acid-neutral soil. H5 / Zones 7–9*

Leaf shape and texture
Annuals and perennials

Herbaceous annuals and perennials make up the bulk of garden plants. They are, on the whole, smaller than trees and many shrubs, and usually die back in winter. Add those with strong patterns to your designs for a solid enhancement of a patchwork of plants. Grow the plants in groups and the pattern can be extended over a larger area.

VERONICASTRUM VIRGINICUM "FASCINATION"

In terms of pattern, "Fascination" has the lot. Whorls of leaves and small flower spikes on rigid stems lead to a vertical purple flower spike that in this cultivar distorts into unusual shapes.

↑ *Perennial, 5 ft (1.5 m) tall, 3¼ ft (1 m) wide. Full sun to part shade. Soil moist, well drained. H7 / Zones 3–8*

DRYOPTERIS AFFINIS "CRISTATA THE KING"

The crested edges of the fronds give them the appearance of a ladder, with strong vertical and horizontal lines.

↑ *Evergreen perennial, 3¼ ft (1 m) tall, 3¼ ft (1 m) wide. Shade to sun. Soil constantly damp. H5 / Zones 4–8*

ATHYRIUM FILIX-FEMINA "FRIZELLIAE"

All ferns have strongly patterned fronds, but "Frizelliae" offers even more, with its pinnae reduced to alternating rounded lobes, like delicate beads.

← *Deciduous perennial, 12 in. (30 cm) tall, 12 in. (30 cm) wide. Shade. Soil damp, acid to neutral. H6 / Zones 4–8*

AEONIUM "LOGAN ROCK"

Succulent, shiny near-black leaves and a tightly packed green center form a great focal point in pots or repeated through a border.

↓ Evergreen perennial, 3¼ ft (1 m) tall, 3¼ ft (1 m) wide. Full sun. Soil free draining. H1c / Zone 11

LEONOTIS NEPETIFOLIA

Tall towers with whorls of orange tubular flowers appear at intervals along the stem. This creates strong vertical lines, while the flowers make a floating pattern of orange pom-poms at the backs of borders.

↓ Perennial, annual in cooler climates, 6 ft (1.8 m) tall, 12 in. (30 cm) wide. Full sun. Soil moist. H1c / Zones 9–11

EQUISETUM HYEMALE

Rigid vertical stems of green with bands of black at equal intervals produce a distinctly precise pattern.

↓ Perennial, 5 ft (1.5 m) tall, 8 in. (20 cm) wide. Full sun to shade. Soil moist. H7 / Zones 3–11

HELIANTHUS SALICIFOLIUS

An incredible sunflower, grown mainly for its often vertical towers of narrow linear foliage arranged like long shaggy brooms down multiple stems.

← Deciduous perennial, 8 ft (2.5 m) tall, 3¼ ft (1 m) wide. Full sun. Soil free-draining alkaline to neutral. H5 / Zones 4–9

Leaf shape and texture
Ground covers

Underrated but essential in any successful garden design, ground covers spread to fill large areas of soil while also preventing weeds. Choose those plants with pattern and the area they colonize will provide year-round interest, thanks to their blanket of texture and shape.

ASARUM EUROPAEUM

Beautiful shiny evergreen leaves of equal size, shaped like an ear, spread gradually to produce a patterned carpet of leaves.

→ *Evergreen, 4 in. (10 cm) tall, unlimited spread. Full to partial shade. Soil fertile, moist, neutral to acid. H6 / Zones 4–8*

EPIMEDIUM PINNATUM SUBSP. COLCHICUM

In spring, dainty ethereal spikes of flowers emerge, followed by ground-smothering, symmetrical leaves, like overlapping feathers.

↓ *Evergreen, 12 in. (30 cm) tall, unlimited spread. Partial shade. Soil moist, well drained, acid to neutral. H7 / Zones 5–8*

ROSMARINUS OFFICINALIS PROSTRATUS

Due to its prostrate growth habit, this rosemary will droop down over walls, creating a lined pattern accentuated by its narrow needle foliage.

↓ *Evergreen, 20 in. (50 cm) tall, 5 ft (1.5 m) wide. Full sun. Soil well drained. H4 / Zones 8–10*

PACHYSANDRA TERMINALIS "GREEN CARPET"

Whorls of serrated evergreen leaves blanket the ground. Each little plant is the same size, forming an even pattern.

↑ *Evergreen, 12 in. (30 cm) tall, unlimited spread. Partial to full shade. Soil well drained. H5 / Zones 4–8*

Leaf shape and texture
Tender plants

In regions affected by frost, tender plants need shelter over winter to survive. Bring them into your home or a heated greenhouse and you'll further increase your range of patterned plants. Grow tender varieties for tropical foliage in exciting shapes and colors.

SOLENOSTEMON "BURGUNDY WEDDING TRAIN"

"Wedding Train" is one of the best examples in a genus where many members have strongly patterned leaves. Its many leaves also create a wider pattern across the plant.

↓ Evergreen, 3¼ ft (1 m) tall, 20 in. (50 cm) wide. Part sun. Growing media moist, well drained. H1c / Zone 11

ALOE POLYPHYLLA

When it comes to plants with a pattern, few can outcompete this perfect spiral.

↑ Evergreen, 12 in. (30 cm) tall, 23½ in. (60 cm) wide. Full sun. Growing media free draining. H3 / Zones 9–12

ASPARAGUS DENSIFLORUS "MEYERSII"

The plant forms dense sprays of green, with leaves in a highly uniform pattern along each fountain-like arching stem.

↑ Evergreen, 20 in. (50 cm) tall, 20 in. (50 cm) wide. Partial shade. Growing media moist, well drained. H1c / Zones 9–11

PILEA PEPEROMIOIDES

Shield-shaped leaves that are as near a perfect circle as any plant leaf. Held on stalks, the leaves form a repeating pattern around the plant, seen from every angle.

← Evergreen, ¼ in. (0.5 cm) tall, ¼ in. (0.5 cm) wide. Partial shade. Growing media well drained. H1c / Zones 9–11

Bark

Many trees and shrubs have beautiful bark. But some take it to another level, mixing color with texture, from rough to shiny smooth, to make striking patterns and add tactile and sculptural interest to your garden.

PRUNUS SERRULA

An ornamental cherry, with prominent lenticels (breathing pores) accentuated by bark that shines like copper.
↓ *Deciduous, 30 ft (9 m) tall, 30 ft (9 m) wide. Full sun. Soil moist but well drained. H6 / Zones 6–8*

ACER CAPILLIPES

A beautiful maple, notable for its green bark, lined vertically from top to bottom, which is stunning year round.
↓ *Deciduous, 39 ft (12 m) tall, 26 ft (8 m) wide. Full sun to part shade. Soil moist but well drained. H6 / Zones 5–7*

CASTANEA SATIVA

The entire length of this large tree carries a swirling pattern of grooves.
↓ *Deciduous, 98 ft (30 m) tall, 66 ft (20 m) wide. Full sun. Well-drained soil, neutral to acidic. H6 / Zones 5–7*

BETULA UTILIS VAR. JACQUEMONTII

Admired for its glowing white bark, *B. utilis* var. *jacquemontii* also has a soft pattern of lenticels.
↑ *Deciduous, 39 ft (12 m) tall, 25 ft (7.5 m) wide. Full sun to part shade. Soil moist but well drained. H7 / Zones 5–7*

LUMA APICULATA

The older branches and stems of this large shrub are coated in a patchwork of cream and downy brown bark.
↑ *Evergreen, 39 ft (12 m) tall, 26 ft (8 m) wide. Full sun to part shade. Soil well drained. H4 / Zones 8–9*

PRUNUS SARGENTII

All cherry trees have lenticels arranged in a horizontal pattern. They are particularly pronounced on *P. sargentii*.
↑ *Deciduous, 30 ft (9 m) tall, 30 ft (9 m) wide. Full sun. Soil moist but well drained. H6 / Zones 4–7*

TRACHYCARPUS FORTUNEI

Its natural coarse woolliness is part of the appeal of *T. fortunei*. But underneath that, the bare trunk reveals a striking striped pattern of ridges formed where old leaves used to grow.

↓ *Evergreen, 26 ft (8 m) tall, 8 ft (2.5 m) wide. Full sun. Soil well drained. H5 / Zones 7–10*

METASEQUOIA GLYPTOSTROBOIDES

As this large conifer matures, its trunk becomes increasingly gnarled into what looks like melted wax, producing a slightly otherworldly appearance.

↑ *Deciduous, 164 ft (50 m) tall, 66 ft (20 m) wide. Full sun. Soil poorly drained. H7 / Zones 4–8*

BETULA ALBOSINENSIS "RED PANDA"

The bark of "Red Panda" has clearly visible horizontal lenticels, and its color, ranging from red to light beige, changes in patches throughout the year and as it grows.

↓ *Deciduous, 49 ft (15 m) tall, 33 ft (10 m) wide. Full sun to part shade. Soil moist but well drained. H7 / Zones 4–7*

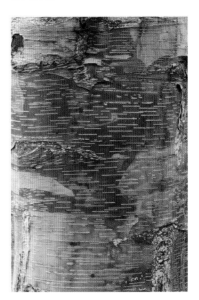

PINUS SYLVESTRIS

Mature examples of *P. sylvestris* have cracked bark, which creates a beautiful abstract pattern. For a more compact form, see *P. sylvestris* "Watereri."

↑ *Evergreen, 59 ft (18 m) tall, 39 ft (12 m) wide. Full sun. Soil well drained. H7 / Zones 3–7*

RUBUS COCKBURNIANUS

A brilliant white dusty bloom makes the stems of this prickly shrub stand out in winter when the leaves have fallen, highlighting its repeated arching pattern.

↑ *Deciduous, 13 ft (4 m) tall, 13 ft (4 m) wide. Full sun. Soil moist but well drained. H6 / Zones 6–7*

Architectural shape
Verticals

For tall punctuation points in a garden, grow plants with vertical shape. Height, combined with a narrow footprint, draws attention because the gravity-defying plants look ready to fall over. Dotted around a garden they will form a larger pattern, with their repetition drawing the eye—or plant them together as an informal hedge.

SEMIARUNDINARIA FASTUOSA

One of the most vertical bamboos, tall with short side branches, *S. fastuosa* spreads, but less than other species.
↑ *Evergreen, 26 ft (8 m) tall, 10 ft (3 m) wide. Full sun to part shade. Soil moist loam but well drained. H6 / Zones 6–7*

CALAMAGROSTIS X ACUTIFLORA

A bolt upright tall grass, with flowers from late summer that hold to the plant all through winter.
↑ *Deciduous, 5 ft (1.5 m) tall, 28 in. (70 cm) wide. Full sun to part shade. Soil well drained. H6 / Zones 5–9*

DIGITALIS FERRUGINEA

Small, rust-colored flowers adorn this foxglove with tall, chest-to-head-height vertical stems that remain as seedpods.
↑ *Semievergreen, 5 ft (1.5 m) tall, 20 in. (50 cm) wide. Full sun to shade. Soil moist but well drained. H6 / Zones 4–8*

CUPRESSUS SEMPERVIRENS "PYRAMIDALIS"

One of the best-known trees for creating "punctuation" in gardens because of its tall, upright form.
↓ *Evergreen, 98 ft (30 m) tall, 16½ ft (5 m) wide. Full sun. Soil well drained. H5 / Zones 7–10*

ECHIUM PININANA

Huge panicles of flowers are produced at remarkable speed in this biennial's second or third year.
→ *Evergreen, 13 ft (4 m) tall, 3¼ ft (1 m) wide. Full sun. Soil well drained. H3 / Zones 9b–10a*

Architectural shape
Horizontals

Add plants with horizontal elements, whether flowers, branches, or leaves, to create flat plates of pattern that bring solidity of structure to a group planting. The pattern changes depending on where you stand as you look at it—from above, a block of color, at a distance, a series of flat lines.

ACHILLEA MILLEFOLIUM "SALMON BEAUTY"

A vigorous, terracotta-colored perennial with horizontal flower heads held rigidly upright through summer and into winter as the flowers fade to seed heads.

← *Deciduous, 32 in. (80 cm) tall, 32 in. (80 cm) wide. Full sun. Soil well drained. H7 / Zones 3–9*

HYDRANGEA ASPERA VILLOSA GROUP

Large shrubs that carry flowers from summer to fall, creating a strong series of horizontal lines.

↑ *Deciduous, 8 ft (2.5 m) tall, 8 ft (2.5 m) wide. Part shade to full sun. Soil well drained, acid-neutral. H5 / Zones 7–10*

ANTHRISCUS SYLVESTRIS

Many umbellifers—plants with discs of tiny flowers—fit the bill of creating strong horizontal accents, and *A. sylvestris* is one of the easiest to grow. Alternative species of umbellifers include *Ammi majus*, *Daucus carota*, and *Foeniculum vulgare*.

↑ *Semievergreen, 5 ft (1.5 m) tall, 3¼ ft (1 m) wide. Part sun. Soil well drained. H6 / Zones 7–10*

HYLOTELEPHIUM SPECTABILE

Many plants in the *Hylotelephium* genus grow large flat heads of flowers for summer and fall color atop stocky stems. They can be made shorter and more branched, and thereby more sturdy, by cutting back by a third to a half in midspring.

↑ *Deciduous, 20 in. (50 cm) tall, 20 in. (50 cm) wide. Full sun. Soil well drained, alkaline to neutral. H7 / Zones 3–9*

Architectural shape
Fountains

Plants that grow in a fountain shape generally have a clear pattern, with their branches, leaves, or flowers spreading evenly from a central point. These plants are good mixers, mingling with others to soften combinations of vertical and horizontal plants. Their conspicuous structure also makes a great focal point.

HAKONECHLOA MACRA

Look to the *Hakonechloa* tribe for low fountains of ground cover. Their leaves, although deciduous, can be left on through winter to add some structure.
↑ *Deciduous, 20 in. (50 cm) tall, 20 in. (50 cm) wide. Full sun to part shade. Soil moist but well drained. H7 / Zones 5–9*

BUDDLEIA DAVIDII "SANTANA"

A striking cultivar of buddleia, with lime-green variegated leaves and magenta spikes of flowers in a strong fountain through most of summer. Prune in late winter to contain size.
↓ *Deciduous, 10 ft (3 m) tall, 10 ft (3 m) wide. Full sun. Soil well drained. H6 / Zones 5–9*

BRAHEA ARMATA

Palms are perfect for a large-scale fountain of foliage, and *B. armata* offers particularly beautiful silver leaves.
↑ *Evergreen, 39 ft (12 m) tall, 13 ft (4 m) wide. Full sun. Soil well drained. H1c / Zones 9–11*

PHORMIUM TENAX

Phormiums all grow in fountain shapes, with either straight or drooping foliage.
↑ *Evergreen, 30 in. (75 cm) tall, 20 in. (50 cm) wide. Full sun. Soil fertile, moist but well drained. H5 / Zones 9–11*

PENNISETUM ALOPECUROIDES "HAMELN"

Many grasses—*Pennisetum* varieties included—grow in a fountain shape. "Hameln"—a shorter variety than most—is extremely reliable for borders.
↑ *Evergreen, 3¼ ft (1 m) tall, 3¼ ft (1 m) wide. Full sun. Soil well drained. H3 / Zones 5–9*

DIERAMA PULCHERRIMUM

Not grown enough, *Dierama* varieties have almost grasslike fountain foliage. In summer, they produce long fishing rodlike stems so narrow it's hard to believe they are strong enough to carry the flowers. Round, dangling seedpods remain long after the flowers have faded.
↑ *Evergreen, 5 ft (1.5 m) tall, 5 ft (1.5 m) wide. Full sun. Soil well drained. H4 / Zones 7–10*

INDIGOFERA HETERANTHA

A shrub that grows and flowers into a beautiful fountain. You can prune it in a similar way to buddleias to contain its size.
↑ *Deciduous, 8 ft (2.5 m) tall, 8 ft (2.5 m) wide. Full sun. Soil moist but well drained. H5 / Zones 7–9*

Architectural shape
Clouds

It may be hard to imagine, but frothy, soft, and fuzzy plants do contain pattern. Look carefully, and it's there—subtle, muted, almost subliminal—in the minute details of the many leaves and flowers. Cloud-like plants produce a kind of relaxed order that makes your garden calmer and more inviting.

MOLINIA CAERULEA SUBSP. ARUNDINACEA "TRANSPARENT"

As the plant's name suggests, the flowers are so lightweight that you can almost see through them—perfect for adding soft texture to any garden area.

↑ *Deciduous, 3¼ ft (1 m) tall, 3¼ ft (1 m) wide. Full sun. Soil moist but well drained. H7 / Zones 5–8*

COTINUS COGGYGRIA

A well-structured shrub that in summer produces panicles of soft, fluffy flowers. As part of a border, or even in the middle of a meadow, the plant creates the impression of a large, pink-tinged cloud.

↑ *Deciduous, 19½ ft (6 m) tall, 16½ ft (5 m) wide. Full sun. Soil moist but well drained. H5 / Zones 5–8*

FOENICULUM VULGARE

Similar to varieties in the *Ammi* genus but with yellow flowers and a prolonged foliage stage that combines well with other plants. The "Purpureum" cultivar has purple-bronze foliage.

← *Deciduous, 6 ft (1.8 m) tall, 32 in. (80 cm) wide. Full sun. Soil well drained to moist. H5 / Zones 4–9*

CALAMAGROSTIS BRACHYTRICHA

A fountain of foliage on this grass makes way for waist-to-chest-high flowers with a particularly open and airy structure.

↑ *Deciduous, 5 ft (1.5 m) tall, 3¼ ft (1 m) wide. Full sun to part shade. Soil moist but well drained. H6 / Zones 4–9*

Architectural shape
Abstract

Some plants look haphazard, yet from their random nature an abstract pattern emerges, thanks to the regularity of their leaves or stems. Use such abstract plants for an informal design—perfect when the plant is repeated—to build a pattern that feels more natural. The mind recognizes the obvious similarities in the plants even if they all grow a little differently.

RICINUS COMMUNIS

Grown in temperate climates as an annual, this shrub, known as the castor oil plant, quickly forms an abstract and alien shape, with large palmate leaves up to 20 in. (50 cm) across and clusters of spiky seedpods. All parts of the plant are toxic, if ingested.
↑ *Evergreen, 8 ft (2.5 m) tall, 6½ ft (2 m) wide. Full sun. Soil well drained. H2 / Zones 8–11*

MELIANTHUS MAJOR

A shrub that has architectural silvery foliage in an expanding mound of sharply cut leaves. Look for the similar species *M. villosus* for a refined alternative.
↓ *Evergreen, 3¼ ft (1 m) tall, 3¼ ft (1 m) wide. Full sun. Soil well drained. H3 / Zones 8–10*

OPUNTIA ENGELMANNII TARDOSPINA F. INERME

The pads of this fairly hardy cactus grow in all directions, creating an unusual statuesque form.
← *Evergreen, 5 ft (1.5 m) tall, 5 ft (1.5 m) wide. Full sun. Soil well drained, gravelly. H3 / Zones 9–10*

PSEUDOPANAX FEROX

The vertical trunk of this tree is adorned with strange, tough black leaves that are sharp to the touch. Like a giant, living pipe cleaner, it eventually matures into a distinct lollipop shape on tall trunks.
↑ *Evergreen, 26 ft (8 m) tall, 6½ ft (2 m) wide. Full sun. Soil well drained sandy, loam. H4 / Zones 8–9*

3

PATTERNS
IN GARDEN
LAYOUTS

The layout of your garden will define its areas, impacting how it's used and what it eventually looks like as a 3-D space—it's the skeleton that underpins everything. Use pattern in the foundation of your garden design to achieve a reassuring sense of order and structure, even in the wildest of gardens.

Symmetrical layouts

Symmetry inherently forms a pattern, as lines and shapes reflect and repeat, relating to one another in varying degrees of complexity. A symmetrical layout has high design impact and appeals to a sense of order that we are programed by evolution to recognize.

When something is mirrored exactly, the resulting shape is said to be symmetrical. Quite why a symmetrical layout feels so impactful may be a reaction to an unnatural-looking garden—no space in nature is exactly symmetrical—or because we are instinctively drawn to symmetry in nature, such as in faces and the wings of a butterfly. For whatever reason, when a garden layout is symmetrical it's guaranteed to elicit an instant "wow" from visitors.

The sense of order created by a symmetrical layout also allows you to easily read an area to better understand where everything is, where you should look and even where you should walk. When you are in one area of a symmetrical garden, the mind subconsciously builds a map of the mirrored layout, helping you, in a small way, to navigate the space.

Symmetry doesn't occur only when a garden is mirrored down a central axis. You can split your garden into as many axes as you wish. Hexagonal and octagonal courtyard and garden layouts have used rotational symmetry for centuries, where each segment is a rotated copy of the other, like the slices of a cake. You can also use a diagonal axis, reflecting the layout across opposing corners, helping to order your garden—but with a marginally less obvious symmetry—and create something that's less rigid and more relaxed.

SYMMETRY AND FRAMEWORK

Château de Villandry in France (left) uses a detailed symmetrical pattern for a parterre layout, exaggerated by the exact mirroring of every plant and detail. Ham House in Richmond, London (right), has a diagonally symmetrical layout but includes a nonsymmetrical checkerboard planting design. Both approaches are equally valid as a way to combine layout pattern and planting.

SYMMETRY AND PERSPECTIVE

Gardens with symmetrical layouts are usually, but not always, found paired with symmetrical architecture, which helps create a sense of unity. On the left, some horticultural flair has been used to enhance a symmetrical layout, using seasonal pots and mirrored topiary. Symmetrical patterns can also heighten perspective lines, as at Scampston Hall in North Yorkshire, UK (above), concentrating your gaze or framing focal points.

Asymmetrical layouts

Many modern gardens have an irregular shape and so demand an asymmetrical layout, where different areas are not mirror images of each other. Spaces in nature are rarely symmetrical, so an asymmetrical layout can feel particularly relaxed and informal.

It's harder to introduce pattern into the layout of an asymmetrical garden because elements aren't necessarily repeated. Instead, pattern is usually added later through planting and landscaping materials to bring order or an interesting feature into the garden. With some thought, though, you can create asymmetrical patterns in layout that will improve the look of your garden. Examples of these include the repetition of a shape, such as circles or squares in different sizes; a specific patterned detail, such as the zigzag of a flight of steps; an overall abstract pattern; or simple touches, such as curves on the corners of planting areas. In essence, the asymmetrical approach is more about creating unity through one linking theme or adding a detail for increased design interest.

For an asymmetrical garden to feel right, it needs good visual balance (see page 24). A square patio next to a circular lawn is obviously an asymmetrical layout, but if the two elements are roughly the same size, they will balance. Also, a dominant stone pathway can be balanced by bold adjacent planting. Consider the size of areas in relation to one another as this will make the difference between the space feeling right or not, which can be tricky to get right on asymmetrical layouts.

SHAPE-LED LAYOUTS

The garden above has a strong abstract pattern layout formed of sharp-line walkways and quadrangle patios, pools, and planting zones. A softer circular layout for a patio and lawn brings relaxed style to the garden above right. These gardens carry the pattern in the layout into the 3-D plane by using angular sculpture and rounded shrubs.

INTRIGUING VIEWS

Even in a small space (opposite), an asymmetrical layout helps to add a sense of movement and expectation, as steps wind in a short zigzag through the garden to a partially obscured seating area. Although the landscaping on the right is modern and clean, the blocklike pattern layout helps the planting to look naturalistic, as house meets the wild.

Abstract patterns

One of the most dramatic garden design trends to emerge in the early 21st century has been the use of bold, abstract pattern in garden layouts. In practice, this is a complex mixture of symmetry, asymmetry, balance, and perspective combined with modern ideas for naturalistic planting, landscaping, and the understanding of space.

Although some abstract garden layouts are symmetrical, most are asymmetrical but with a strong sense of balance across the individual areas. For instance,

Dutch garden designer and plantsperson Piet Oudolf is known for his perennial meadow plantings that are often formed of abstract island planting areas with paths running around them. This can be seen on the High Line (right) in New York City, where a disused railway line has been turned into a planted "greenway."

Although none of the islands are the same shape, they balance one another and create a sense of unity. Often this is because each has an equal area (whether a square or a triangle), or because

together they form a larger shape, such as a giant triangle consisting of all the beds, the overall form of which becomes clear when viewed from a distance.

In Milan, Italy, Dutch architect Petra Blaisse's garden installation *Library of Trees* (left), which opened in 2018, uses a combination of "islands" of lawn and planting divided by paths. The planting and lawn areas are linked by their similar angular shape and roughly the same visual weighting in terms of area. A secondary pattern layer of circular forests sits over the top of the angular grid.

In abstract garden design, the primary pattern almost always comes from the layout of the garden itself. Usually this pattern can be appreciated from raised viewpoints, such as adjacent buildings. But the design serves a purpose on the ground, too. The abstract pattern creates feelings of calm—because the space feels natural—and adventure, as you explore around each corner, not knowing what will come next.

With the layout forming the core pattern from which everything else hangs, the hard landscaping is often minimalist, using only a few materials to create clean lines to frame what can be highly complicated matrix plantings. These plantings are usually naturalistic in style, inspired by nature—though not necessarily mimicking it. Low-maintenance prairies, perennial meadows, and woodland-style plantings with year-round interest are all made possible thanks to the simplicity of the overall design.

Usability is the main consideration in abstract pattern layouts. On New York City's High Line (above), people can walk freely along a path cutting diagonally across an area free from restrictive design formalities. Planting areas with abstract shapes contribute to the feel of nature reclaiming the city, enhanced by the ridge pattern of the edging.

Although most designers opt for naturalistic or partially naturalistic planting for abstract layouts, it doesn't have to be that way. The *Library of Trees* in Milan (left) encompasses areas of naturalistic planting alongside regimented areas with formal repetitions of trees.

Formal layouts

Layouts with an obvious pattern are common to formal gardens, where clean lines, structure, and order are the key. Here, the layout rules the roost—clearly visible and giving a garden purpose and theater.

Pattern lends itself to a formal design because a precise pattern in a natural space is rare and obviously human-made; think of the difference between a natural forest and a strictly controlled planted forest. Repetition, too, is a common feature of a formal layout, adding to the drama and sense of occasion.

A formal layout might include alcoves in walls for pots or statuary, repeated segments of lawn divided by paths, and boundaries, such as walls or hedged perimeters. Planting areas repeated in matching shapes, with paths weaving through or around them, build formality, too, as do perfectly proportioned raised beds in a kitchen garden. Paths in formal layouts are wide and prominent, leading from home to outdoor seating areas, perhaps with large planting areas alongside. Everything is later enhanced with high-quality materials, furniture, and structures that add to the feel of the garden. But above all, in formal gardens it's the layout that remains the star.

GRAND STATEMENTS

Piet Oudolf's "Drifts of Grass" area at Scampston Hall in North Yorkshire, UK (above), is undeniably a formal garden, but not in the traditional sense. Mass plantings of *Mollinia* "Poul Petersen" wave repeatedly through the large space, surrounding only four chairs, in an almost symmetrical fashion, either side of a grand path. It's relaxing but intended to impress.

SIGNS OF FORMALITY

In a relatively small private garden (left), a formal garden has been created from a simple asymmetrical layout with clearly designated paths and covered seating area, enhanced by repetition in planting and containers. On a grander scale, repeating rows of lollipop topiary, immaculate grass, and circular windows in a hedge (right) make for an ambitiously formal garden.

FORMAL SELF-SUFFICIENCY

When you think of growing fruit and veg, messy allotments may spring to mind.
But there is another way. Kitchen gardens have a long history in the formal
design of stately homes, and you don't need bags of cash to recreate the look.
The above garden feels formal thanks to a neat and tidy layout enhanced by
gravel paths and raised beds edged with painted wood.

Informal layouts

Seen as a plan on paper, an informal garden layout can look much like a formal one. But look closely and there will be some obvious signs of informality, including less regimented pattern. It could be time to throw formal grandeur over the garden fence.

Space in an informal garden is notably smaller and more intimate than in open formal gardens, producing a private and enclosed feel. Large gardens can be divided up into smaller areas for an informal layout, perhaps with meandering paths—narrower than formal designs—that encourage you to take time to wander, both physically and mentally.

Shapes play a role, with circles, wriggles, and gentle curves instantly making a space feel softer. Geometric shapes and straight lines can still feel informal if used in a more abstract overall pattern or when you know the planting will soften the edges, perhaps by growing over them. Overall, the feel of an informal design is relaxed and playful, but still practical.

TRADITIONAL LOOK

There are no holds barred in the lavish planting in Lytes Cary Manor gardens, Somerset, UK (above and left). And yet these are clearly informal garden layouts. Beyond the planting, which breaks with the rigid repetition and symmetry of formal gardens, clues in the layout include narrow paths and areas enclosed within tall screening hedges, creating a sense of intimacy.

ADDING INFORMALITY

A small modern garden with clean lines (right) feels informal thanks to its layout. A curved path drifts through planting, and low walls, doubling as seats, break up the space into different areas. Another modern garden (below) uses generous planting areas to soften the paving and walls.

RELAXED EXOTICA

Tropical planting was traditionally used in formal bedding schemes, but contemporary use leans toward a more relaxed, informal appearance. In the garden on the left, the lack of paths or paving gives visitors the freedom to walk wherever they wish.

Patterns in fantastic modern plantings

Contemporary planting design is a fusion of past styles, combining mixed borders, naturalism, and structure, with pattern playing an exciting role. Whether intentional or not, pattern in modern planting is everywhere, from leaf shape to the mix and spacing of colors.

Pattern lets you create truly adventurous combinations while helping to unify everything in a formation that guarantees unity and the wow factor. Plant choices then allow you to adjust the pattern impact up or down.

The fastest way of adding pattern to a planting scheme is to introduce a plant with a visually strong patterned habit or leaf (see pages 30–47), such as a variegated *Solenostemon*, a fountain of *Cordyline australis* "Pink Passion" foliage, or the structured branches of *Aralia echinocaulis*. Put too many of these patterned plants

Gravetye Manor (below), in Sussex, UK, may be a 400-year-old manor but head gardener Tom Coward and team are certainly not stuck in the past with their planting layouts. Colorful modern cultivars of perennials, shrubs, and annuals repeat across the garden in an exciting fusion of naturalism and planned extravagance.

At Parham Gardens (left), in Sussex, UK, yellow-themed borders demonstrate the perfect use of patterns in shape and form with massed verticals of *Verbascum* species, horizontal achilleas, and fountains of *Stipa gigantea*.

An extraordinary planting pattern (below) at Hunting Brook Gardens in Ireland makes innovative use of color and form in combining bright orange marigolds and woolly cacti, among other plants.

together, though, and they can start to look unnatural and jarring. To minimize this, position strongly patterned plants apart, separated by more relaxed species, such as salvias, geranium, or ornamental grasses. Mix pattern as you would bold colors or differently shaped foliage; some plants will be focal points and others filler.

A repeated plant combination is another way of adding pattern to a planting scheme. Exact repetition of the same combination along a border is the most visually striking pattern, grabbing your attention and then pulling it through the repeated elements like words in a sentence, the mind recognizing pattern as it would punctuation. Repeating combinations in a different order, or repeating colors and shapes using different plants, can build patterns, too, but in a more relaxed, less striking way.

When planting on a bigger scale over large areas, such as in public parks, the pattern is often scaled up by planting in bold blocks of the

same plant. This is similar to the way pattern is used in a parterre (see pages 96–7), but with relaxed-looking plants instead of clipped hedges and topiary.

The Great Broad Walk Borders at Kew Gardens, in London, use all these techniques in one go. The entire layout is broken down into huge semicircular beds flanking the more than 1,050 ft (320 m) long walk, each made of a patterned layout that's mirrored within each semicircle and then again on the

opposite side. Each set of semicircles has a different pattern, using perennials punctuated by topiary yew pyramids.

Next time you are adding plants to your garden, perhaps for a border overhaul, or starting a new scheme, consider the many ways of using pattern with plants. Experiment by placing plants next to each other before planting and then focus on the patterns you are creating. Also think about plant combinations that mix shape and form.

4

PATTERNS USING PLANTS

Arranging plants in a beautiful way is one of the founding principles of garden design—and it's also incredibly satisfying. As soon as you get going, you'll not only be pruning and training but also designing plant patterns, building rhythm, and creating color and texture combinations.

Simple repetition

Repeating the color or shape of a plant instantly transforms a garden, whatever its size—and it's easy to do this in containers or along the edges of flowerbeds. One beautiful plant on a balcony or patio, for instance, enhances the space, but three of the same plants in a row—well, that's striking.

There are many ways you can repeat plants in a garden. Spacing them equally looks smart and stylish, but being more relaxed with the repetition will make the space feel relaxed, too. Try different plants with the same flower color, or exactly the same plants but spaced unevenly; use different plants with a similar structure, and even repeat the same plant but in different sizes. Your eye will pick up the similarities more than the differences, linking them into a repetition pattern. Have fun repeating plants, and even try mixing multiple repetitions together to discover what different patterns you can achieve.

POTS

Not only are they practical plant holders, pots can also look really attractive—even more so when partnered with the right plant. Try repeating the same plant and pot in a row (below), at the corners of a patio, lining the sides of a path or attached to a wall (above). Or go wild and group lots of pots together for a more intricate pattern (left). You can use almost any kind of plant, from flowering plants and ornamental grasses, to succulents and evergreen foliage.

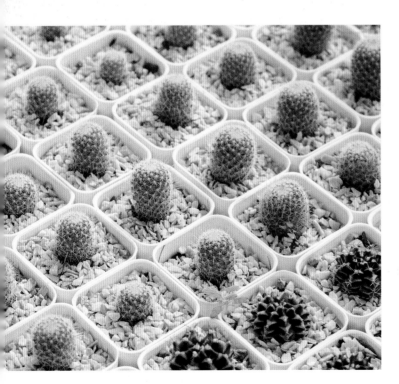

WINDOW BOXES

Thanks to window boxes, everyone can grow plants—garden or no garden. One of the simplest window box patterns is to repeat the same plants along the box or trough, either alternating them or by planting symmetrically, with a central focal plant and companions mirrored either side. Then take things to the next level by repeating the window box across all the windows of a building (left).

PLANTING AREAS

Dotting plants around a planted area can help to give it structure and visual intrigue as the repetition draws the eye from one plant to the next. If everything is repeated equally, the area can feel ordered and neat, while mixing things up a bit generates excitement and a more natural-looking feel. Repetition doesn't have to be exact; using *Rudbeckia fulgida* var. *deamii* at the front of a planting area (right), with the taller *Rudbeckia triloba* at the back, still creates repetition from the similarly colored flowers, even though they are different species.

Combinations

Thinking about how plants complement and interact with one another takes time. But it's one of the most rewarding aspects of gardening, which will repay you with greater beauty and often surprising results. Think of combinations as small pieces of pattern within the larger garden tapestry.

In designed planting schemes, including areas you've planted gradually through the years, most plants, rather than just one or two, are repeated. In fact, it's the stand-alone focal plants that are usually the exception. To make order of what could be planting chaos—and for a border to look esthetically pleasing—use the idea of plant groups, or combinations.

There are an unlimited number of combinations you can grow, but to get started, think about mixing plants that have different colors, shape, structure, and texture. Do this, and a group of plants will be more interesting to look at and feel more structured.

COLORFUL COMBINATIONS

With such a wide variety of plants available today, the world of combinations is your oyster. In spring, tulips (above) growing through a mass of forget-me-nots (*Myosotis sylvatica*) is a classic, as the blue flowers hide the leaves, while the tulips rise to flower above them. For continued color from summer into fall, look to late-season performers such as *Hylotelephium* "Purple Emperor" and *Helenium* "Sahin's Early Flowerer," as well as varieties of *Echinacea*, *Persicaria*, and *Symphyotrichum*.

TEXTURED COMBINATIONS

Lush foliage plants, such as *Matteuccia struthiopteris*, *Astelia chathamica*, *Brachyglottis greyi*, and towering *Pseudopanax* species (left), create layers of texture. Grasses are also perfect for creating softer texture, including *Jarava ichu* and *Miscanthus* "Gracillimus" in sun, or *Hakonechloa* species in shade.

PLAYING WITH REPETITION

A combination of plants repeated the length of a planting area can make a dramatic, less natural pattern. Below, repeated sculpted yew hedging in equal-sized segments filled with *Nepeta* species and masses of alliums lead the eye to a water feature and beyond.

Try a subtle change each time you repeat a combination. Your eye will subconsciously pick up on the repetition of key plants, shapes, and colors, tying everything into the pattern. At Ulting Wick in Essex, UK, owner Philippa Burrough has created two sets of tropical pots using the same plants but in a slightly altered arrangement (right). At first, the pots appear to be mirrored, but look closely and there are noticeable differences, adding a dash of artistic flair.

SWEEPS AND SWATHES

By planting more than one of any particular plant, you can group them into blocks or lines, or loop them around each other. Above, the different shapes of *Kniphofia* "Alcazar" (red-hot poker), *Achillea* "Walther Funcke," and *Dahlia* "Pathfinder" create a striking pattern. On the right, *Echinops ritro* "Veitch's Blue," *Perovskia atriplicifolia* "Little Spire," and *Gaura* "Whirling Butterflies" produce a pattern that's soft, mixing shape and form.

MIXING IT UP

Shrubs, grasses, perennials, and annuals all bring something different to the party, and by combining them you can create a rich pattern with a long season. On the left, the ornamental grass *Calamagrostis brachytricha* lays down a soft, vertical, slightly arching texture in front of a block of pale blue *Symphyotrichum*, which has picked up the color baton from summer-flowering *Helenium* and *Monarda* in front. Grasses, in particular, look magical in soft fall sun.

Mixed plantings also let you play with height. Above, partially transparent white spires of *Veronicastrum virginicum* "Album" in the foreground allow light through to shorter *Echinacea purpurea*, with taller *Eupatorium purpureum* (loved by butterflies) shielding what's behind, to be revealed as you walk around the garden. Think about changing height through the season as plants grow.

COMBINATIONS OF FORM

Sculptural plants, such as *Agave attenuata* and *Echinocactus grusonii* (below), have patterns to their form and shape that repeat each time the plant is used. Combined, they create a vivid array of shape and texture. Other plants for this planting style include palms for sun and ferns for shade.

Combinations in naturalistic planting

In nature, a plant tends to spread fairly close to its parent, gradually forming combinations with other plants in an ad hoc, delightful pattern. Naturalistic planting allows you to emulate or reflect the most beautiful-looking elements of plants in the wild.

When you visit a woodland or meadow, or simply look at a roadside verge, you'll see the same plants repeated in clumps and swathes, or simply dotted about. Sometimes there are hundreds of different species of plants, at other times only a handful. Patterns are revealed in the way the plants spread. In California's Mojave Desert (below), for example, Joshua trees (*Yucca brevifolia*) are naturally spaced at almost perfect intervals with species of cacti and conifers

between them. This natural spacing of plants can be the result of competition from other plants, grazing and other disruption from animals, or the distance a plant spreads or casts its seeds.

Garden designers have long marveled at the patterns formed by nature, wanting to embrace some of its serendipitous magic. You cannot recreate wild planting exactly, but through naturalistic planting you'll capture at least some of its drama and spirit.

SUN AND SHADE

Airy grassy plantings, such as the froth of
buff *Nassella tenuissima* (pony tail grass)
on the right, contrasting with the purple
spires of *Salvia nemorosa* "Caradonna," are
synonymous with naturalistic designs. Grass
comes in myriad forms, shades, and sizes.
Good grasses for sunny situations include
Deschampsia cespitosa "Goldtau," and
Molinia caerulea "Transparent."

   Plants grow wild in all situations,
including the shade beneath woodland
canopies. Above, British designer Sarah
Eberle has used a lively mix of shade-
loving plants, such as *Silene dioica* (red
campion), *Lychnis flos-cuculi* (ragged robin),
Dryopteris erythrosora, and *Geranium
himalayense* "Gravetye."

NATURAL FORMS

Dense, untamed naturalistic planting benefits
from juxtaposed hard landscaping and furniture.
On the left, a wooden walkway, with clean lines
and simple style, cuts through the planting to
frame what would otherwise be quite a fairly
loose, unstructured planting design.

ATMOSPHERE

The appeal of naturalistic style is to build an atmospheric escape that's calming but also includes many exciting plants. A fallen tree (opposite, top) adds surprise and interest, especially when plants, such as *Umbilicus rupestris*, start to colonize it, while seating areas allow you to become immersed in the scene (left). Tropical gardens, by their nature, are naturalistic because they try to create a wild jungly feel, with large leaves mingling together and spilling onto paths and seating areas (above).

To achieve a naturalistic look, you can combine plants in much the same way as anywhere else in a garden, but always with an eye for what captures the atmosphere of nature. Don't worry if a plant flops into another or grows in an unexpected place. This all adds to the natural appearance.

ARID STYLE

Around the world there are many different kinds of arid landscape, all characterized by tough plants growing in poor, scorched ground. Given the right dry, temperate conditions, you can achieve a pattern of stark background punctuated by lush, drought-resistant growth, as seen in the American desert garden below in Phoenix, Arizona. Low plants build a pattern of yellow dots around a gravel path leading to shrubs, trees, cacti, and agave behind.

Naturalistic planting in modern landscaping

Wild plant communities are an explosion of striking, natural pattern that shift and change with time. Bring this beautiful tussle into your garden and you'll enjoy plants alive with seasonal magic.

Many garden designers embrace naturalistic planting as an exciting way to emulate the best of the wild in a more contained setting. That's not to say the naturalistic garden is overgrown or uses only wild flowers—it's simply an expression of free-flowing nature captured as plants cohabit in dense plant communities. Perhaps surprisingly, it's these nature-inspired schemes that can display the strongest pattern.

Naturalistic plantings tend to limit the variety of plants used, repeating them through an area either singly or in groups—as you would find in nature. However, such plantings aren't limited in scope and still use broad palettes, particularly for successional color. The plants are set out to create a feel of randomness—or, when started from seed, are genuinely random. Some plants will form verticals, some mounds and clumps, while others spread ground cover. Throughout, an understanding of each plant's life cycle and method of growth over time is critical.

Together, the set of plants creates an elaborate design that, although random, forms a strong pattern as the plants repeat and the mind senses their rhythm. As each plant is repeated, the eye picks up on the random natural pattern. Every combination is different, but because the same set of plants is used, the mind recognizes the combinations as repetition in a pattern. It's as if the stronger-looking plants are the pattern in a wallpaper and the filler plants are the spaces between.

Throughout the seasons and across the years, naturalistic designs will evolve as plants spread, seed, and die. The pattern will shift and move with each year, but it holds together because the palette of plants used is the same. In some years, one plant may dominate, and in others a different plant, creating a refreshing sense of surprise and of a living entity.

Because the density of planting suppresses weed growth, the best naturalistic plantings will be low maintenance. They also offer color and interest through most of the year. Every plant can be chosen according to its seasonal beauty, from fresh new growth in spring to statuesque seed heads in winter. This design approach suits all environments, from manor house to urban estate.

Among naturalistic plantings (below) designed by Nigel Dunnett at the Barbican, in London, domes of acid green *Euphorbia characias* subsp. *wulfenii* dominate the planting in spring, alongside fountains of the low grass *Sesleria nitida*. All will soon be joined by the large globes of *Allium* "Purple Sensation" seen in bud on the left.

The Walled Garden at
Scampston Hall (above),
in North Yorkshire, UK—
seen here in August—shows
the naturalistic approach of
Dutch designer Piet Oudolf,
combining plants at all
stages of life in repeating
natural patterns. Purple
clumps of *Monarda didyma*
"Scorpion" are repeated,
while magenta buttons of
Knautia macedonica are
dotted about through tawny
Deschampsia cespitosa
"Goldtau" grass.

Meadows

A meadow is a form of naturalistic planting where the designer or gardener selects the plants but doesn't choose their exact positions. As in the wild, the design is left entirely to chance as the plants battle it out with one another for space and a moment in the spotlight.

Meadows are rich in pattern. One glance and you'll find a number of dominant grasses and flowers repeated over the entire area, a living pattern emerging and expanding across the ground. Splodges and broad sweeps of plants grow in natural combinations, never evenly spaced but with their repetition building rhythm. Insects love meadows, buzzing, fluttering, and adding a dynamic, living element to the pattern, especially butterflies with their colorful wings.

LARGE-SCALE PATTERN
From a distance, the fine detail of a meadow is like an impressionist painting, with thousands of dots of color, making for a grand and rewarding garden feature. Below, a dominant network of yellow *Hypochaeris radicata* (cat's ear) is interspersed with groups of *Leucanthemum vulgare* (ox-eye daisy), set off by pops of color from *Papaver rhoeas* (poppy).

BACKGROUND FEATURE

Grasses are a core ingredient of any meadow. Ornamental meadows are usually grown on poor soils to keep grasses in check, although they will work on richer soils—it's all about growing the right plant for the conditions. A rough rule of thumb is that annual-based meadows prefer soil of low fertility, while perennial meadows do well in high-fertility soils. A good proportion of native plants is best for wildlife.

SEASONAL SHIFTS

Meadows change throughout the year as one plant comes into flower followed by the next. At Great Dixter Gardens in Sussex, UK (right), airy blooms of *Anthriscus sylvestris* (cow parsley) and the yellow buttons of *Ranunculus acris* (meadow buttercup) fill a spring meadow, with the daffodil *Narcissus poeticus* var. *recurvus* populating the foreground. Later in the year, these will all be overtaken by different flowers.

Bedding

Unlike a meadow, bedding is an unnatural, fully designed feature for maximum impact—and with pattern in its soul. These plantings deserve greater credit for their sheer impact and the joy they invoke, with ample room for modern reinvention.

Traditionally, bedding is created by drawing a pattern or design first, which is transferred into a planting area, using string or spray chalk, and then planted densely with low-growing, colorful specimens packed in so tightly you can't see any soil. These days, bedding is more adventurous, reaching great heights with fast-growing tropicals, while introducing elements of naturalistic design, such as mixing plants to blur lines.

Combine it with modern, environmentally friendly design, and bedding delivers pattern that packs a visual punch. Look on bedding as a framed, living artwork or sculpture in an area where you can let your pattern dreams run wild. Design whatever you want now and then try something different next season.

PATTERNED FOCAL POINTS

In the right location, a designed bedding pattern can be thought of as a living work of art. Below, at the Madeira Botanical Garden, in Funchal, a series of beds have been designed around paths for a supersized patchwork of vibrant color. Bedding often replicates patterns from centuries ago, giving it a dated look, but with some imagination and carefully chosen plants you can create something modern and new.

REPEAT FOR DRAMA

Bedding is all about maximizing the impact—stepping around a corner and being blown away by color and patterned shapes. At Levens Hall, in Cumbria, UK, mass planting of purple verbena edged with neatly clipped *Buxus sempervirens* (left) stretches into the distance, repeated in circles around aged yew trees. Alternatively, rows and blocks of color draw the eye (below left), while an uncomplicated line of tulips (below) forms a simple, elegant pattern in its repeated white flowers.

ENDLESS POSSIBILITIES

Opposite page, clockwise from top left: tightly packed plants frame a path in a large-scale, high-impact modern pattern; tropical beds tower over head height in a more relaxed approach, using patterned forms and shapes, including *Ricinus communis* and *cosmos*; impact and flowing forms combine, with towering *R. communis*, *Verbena bonariensis*, and spiky phormiums, surrounded by drifts of low-lying plants.

This page, clockwise from top: positively exuberant annual bedding displays a white and yellow pattern of *Antirrhinum* "Snapshot F1 White," *Cleome hassleriana* "White Queen," *Euphorbia marginata*, *Nicotiana sylvestris*, *Rudbeckia hirta* "Prairie Sun," *R. hirta* "Toto Lemon," and *Zinnia angustifolia* "Crystal White;" a mass planting of *Pericallis* is edged by variegated foliage repeated in the further bed; at Weihenstephan Gardens, in Germany, towering cannas, dahlias, and grasses create a detailed, symetrical pattern that emphasizes perspective along a path.

Lawn art

Like bedding, lawn art—mowing patterns into grass for a striking but temporary feature—is an old practice that has benefited from some modern thinking. It's not just about stripes—there are so many more possibilities.

Lawn patterns are made by cutting grass at different heights—some areas on the lowest mower setting, some on the highest, and some not cut at all (below). From spirals, curves, and zigzags to full-on mazes (see page 85), you can cut a lawn into whatever pattern you want, even enhancing it with some taller-growing ornamental grasses (right).

Use the narrowest mower you can find—or even a strimmer to make cuts with more detail. Some robot lawn mowers can now be programed to cut patterns, or, if you are feeling particularly athletic, nothing beats a pair of scissors.

Patterns cut into lawns are, by their nature, large-scale features. They are high impact, even in a smaller garden, because lawns tend to use a large space right in the middle. The pattern will be the first thing people see, viewable from most areas of the garden and surrounding buildings.

FLORAL FLOURISHES

Once you have mastered lawn art, experiment with more adventurous patterns, such as flower shapes (above). If a pattern doesn't look right, simply mow everything to erase it and start again when the grass has regrown. Don't just think flowers—choose any shape you like.

STRAIGHT LINES OR CURVES?

Because lawn mowers are roughly square shaped, geometric patterns with straight lines (above) tend to be easier to create. Grids, diamonds, squares, and lines can be marked out with string and then cut with a small mower. Antique push mowers—if you can find one—offer the narrowest cuts.

Spirals, circles, curves, and waves are trickier to cut than straight lines. They are achieved most easily on a large lawn, where longer sweeps can be made with less fiddly turning, depending on mower size. Although time-consuming to cut, a curvy lawn (right) looks softer than one with straight stripes.

Mazes

Who can resist the temptation to explore a maze? It's an exciting human-sized puzzle with a wonderful sense of enclosure as children and adults alike rush around searching for the center or an exit. A pattern that's also a game—what's not to love?

A maze is a superscale pattern in three dimensions. Looking at a maze from above, the pattern becomes obvious from the many different lines of hedging and paths. For centuries, lawns too have been cut into a simple maze pattern, following the same principle but without the raised boundaries. The challenge is to make the pattern complex enough, so that even with full visibility it's hard to guess where the puzzle ends.

When you plan a maze, the experience must come first—those feelings of excitement, fun, mild panic, and reward. A maze must also be enough of a challenge for no one to complete it straight away. Layouts using pattern are particularly useful for this because their repetition can mislead you into thinking your know their shape, when actually some of the paths have been subtly changed to confuse.

HEDGED MAZES

Mazes made from tall hedging are the most familiar (above and right). Their height creates mystery and foreboding because once you enter the maze, you cannot see where you are going or where you have been, and each corner looks the same. Any hedging plant is suitable, although evergreens are best for year-round use. Try *Taxus baccata* (yew), *Lonicera nitida*, or *Prunus laurocerasus* (laurel).

LAWN MAZES

Cutting a maze into a lawn is a more cost-effective approach. You can change the pattern regularly and there's less maintenance because you don't have to look after and trim endless hedges. On the down side, cutting the paths is precise and time-consuming work—and you don't get that feeling of enclosure or the frisson of getting lost. However, lawn mazes can still prove confusing and challenging to complete, especially if you allow barriers of grass between the path to grow long and obscure parts of the basic pattern.

Topiary

Like all plant styles, topiary—the art of clipping shrubs or trees into ornamental shapes—can create pattern through repetition and combination. The shapes themselves also contain pattern, bringing an utterly individual form to a garden.

As topiarized shrubs and hedging are easily sculpted, you can cut any pattern you want into them. Create horizontal, diagonal, or vertical lines and stripes. Cloud prune or add waves, steps, cubes, repeating circles, and floral shapes. Transform a flat hedge from garden backstage to star of the show in a few clean cuts.

A change can be simple, such as a curved top repeated across a few hedges; or it can be much more detailed, with a patterned work of art spread across an entire face. Topiary suits every type of garden, from formal to modern, perhaps ornamenting a parterre or floating above a meadow, its solid shapes contrasting with fluffy grasses.

Topiary can be created from any plant suitable for cutting, such as *Prunus laurocerasus* "Rotundifolia" (cherry laurel), *Laurus nobilis* (bay), and *Griselinia littoralis*. For more detailed pattern, try fine-leaved plants such as *Ligustrum ovalifolium* (privet), *Taxus baccata* (yew), or *Lonicera ligustrina* var. *yunnanensis* (box-leaved honeysuckle).

PATTERN IN 3-D

Topiary is perfect for impactful pattern that can be seen from all angles. Tall cones in the garden above right provide height behind a lower pattern of soft-clipped cushions of *Buxus sempervirens* and mounds of *Hakonechloa macra*. Designer chairs and pond add to the sense of unity. Cloud pruning (right) acknowledges pattern found in nature and exaggerates it for further impact.

LIVING SCULPTURE

At Knightshayes in Devon, UK (above),
topiary statues, mirrored and repeated
in a grid flanking a long path, play with
perspective and focus. In two modern
French topiary interpretations, giant slabs
of hedge at the Jardins de Marqueyssac, in
the Dordogne (right), are set at odd angles,
resembling a living version of a cubist
artwork, while, in Normandy, *Des Gouttes
de pluie* by Spanish artist Samuel Salcedo
(below left), encases sleeping heads in
scallop-patterned hedging. En masse,
topiary always produces pattern and
impact (below right).

Miniature patterns: mosses, succulents, and alpines

Thanks to their small scale and many different colors, shades, and textures, diminutive plants, like moss, succulents, and alpines, present the opportunity for pattern in miniature. Easy to arrange and to change, they are perfect for livening up rock gardens, living walls, and paving.

Principles of pattern for miniature plants are identical to those for bedding—in fact, some bedding schemes use miniatures on a large scale. To get started, you draw a design and then transfer it to the planting spot. This could be a large container—such as a stone trough—a raised bank, between paving, or on a frame, hung, like a picture, on a wall.

Buy in bulk and then plant tightly to ensure there are no gaps between each specimen. Dense planting means the plants will need to be removed and divided each year to avoid overcrowding, although that then gives you the chance to create a new pattern. If you use plants that spread over time, such as *Thymus serpyllum*, *Sempervivum tectorum*, and dwarf *Hylotelephium*, they will knit together better.

GROWING UP

Small succulents and alpines love vertical surfaces because they often grow naturally on cliffs and screes, needing only a small amount of soil to insert their roots. You can recreate these conditions using pots and living wall systems (right), or a wooden frame with a metal wire mesh to hold the compost. Allow the plants to root horizontally before hanging.

EASY PATTERN WINS

Nooks and crannies in a drystone wall filled with some compost make a good home for alpines and succulents (above left). Use tiny examples to make simple patterned table decorations (above right) or to create mini-patterned plantings in gravel and alongside paving. Even an old driveway can be transformed with small ground-cover plants, mosses, and grasses (left). Moss will also add character to any shaded, damp spots.

Living walls and roofs

Gardening is no longer just about gardens. Walls and roofs have opened up radical possibilities for planting around the home. Hundreds of small plants grown tightly together can turn a wall or roof into prime real estate for amazing pattern.

Growing systems for walls consist of planting pockets, about the size of a small pot, closely packed together, with built-in irrigation. Install them inside or out, in sun or shade, using plants that suit these different situations. Living roofs don't have planting pockets. Instead, the plants sit in a waterproof tray, filled with a lightweight growing medium.

    Either way, walls and roofs both use small plants (limited by root space) that, as in bedding, can be planted tightly. By selecting different colors, shapes, and textures, you can plant naturalistically or in artful patterns. When used in built-up areas, living walls and roofs can reduce trapped heat and pollution, as well as provide beautiful breaks in the urban landscape.

VERTICAL PLANTING

Unlike walls smothered in climbing plants, where only one or two plants are used, a living wall can be treated just like a planting area on the ground, with tens, if not hundreds, of different plants combined together, only with a vertical perspective. You can plant a wall like perennial bedding, using carefully selected perennials for year-round patterns, featuring swathes and blocks of different colors and textures (top right). Or treat a wall like a more regular planting area (opposite, top), where it can become a focal point. A wall may be naturalistic—planted like a cliffside—or even consist of large shrubs spread over several storeys (bottom right).

LIFE OVERHEAD

Having no planting pockets, a living roof (left) is slightly more flexible than a living wall. It needs only some shallow soil, with the depth dependent on how much weight the roof can take. A roof can be planted up in the same way as a living wall—either into a designed pattern or allowed to form natural patterns as plants self-seed and spread. Drought-tolerant plants, such as varieties of *Carex*, *Hylotelephium*, and *Sempervivum*, are good choices as they reduce the need for watering.

Renaissance gardens

Between the 14th and 17th centuries in Europe, the explosion in scientific discovery and artistic creativity of the Renaissance pushed forward understanding of nature and the world. It inspired a revolution in gardens, and today the order and beauty of Renaissance patterns remain an inspiration for the ambitious gardener.

The Renaissance began in Italy, where gardens were created for secluded areas to encourage contemplation and relaxation. Hedges and paths were laid out, and clipped low plants, such as herbs and ground cover, were introduced in designed patterns.

Gradually the garden was seen as a tool for demonstrating power and political standing. Italian gardens of the wealthy grew larger, with statues, terraces, and other grand structures. Areas were designed to be viewed from above or from platforms or mounds, increasing the number of patterned layouts created close to buildings.

By the time Renaissance trends reached France, landowners craved grandeur. Garden designs became regimented and were laid out in symmetrical patterns called parterres, intended to reflect the symmetry of buildings. Water too played a role, with elaborate fountains, canals, and ponds dug

out into patterns similar to those of the parterre. The shaping and taming of nature was considered highly civilized and an object lesson in beauty—like a landscape painting on a grand scale.

Originally, patterns created from clipped plants were the main element of parterres, usually filled with colored gravel or sand rather than flowers. Some of the grandest parterres have survived at Château de Villandry in the Loire valley (below), where elaborate designs in immaculately clipped hedges look like living artworks in 3-D.

Renaissance gardens didn't only consist of parterres. Grottoes, statuary, columns, and topiary

The gardens at the Château de Villandry in France (left) have multiple parterres filled with patterns.

At Waterperry Gardens, in Oxfordshire, soft early morning sunlight bathes a modern interpretation of a Renaissance garden (above), where topiary pyramids and pony tail grass (*Nassella tenuissima*) surround a single central statue.

were also recognizable elements. In Britain, an area known as a "wilderness" also featured, inspired by the *bosco* (meaning "wood") feature found in Italian gardens. It was far from "wild," though, its layout planned in a similar way to a parterre, with patterns but using much taller plants for privacy and screening. There are good wilderness examples at Hampton Court Palace and Ham House in the London Borough of Richmond.

It's easy to look at Renaissance gardens today as ostentatious relics of the past, their clipped hedges too austere, their layouts too restricted and unnatural. But it would be wrong to dismiss the use of Renaissance ideas in modern gardens, especially as what we see now is often a slightly misinterpreted restoration. It's better to look to the period for inspiration to reinterpret, such as using large-scale pattern to be viewed from above or immersed in at ground level, and placing statues around the garden as focal points, perhaps as storytelling themes incorporated into the layout—as was popular at the time. And who says the fairytale grotto shouldn't be revived?

Rather than seeing Renaissance design as an open-air museum exhibit, look to the principles and why they existed: freedom of expression, exploring art with plants, story, and excitement, and as an outdoor gallery for statues, fountains, and fine craft. We tend to view Renaissance gardens as constrained, when in fact the opposite may be true.

Knot gardens

Every square, triangle, or circle in a knot garden can be filled with colorful plants in an intricate pattern as unique as you want it to be. Try a modern take on an age-old traditional feature.

Knot gardens were first recorded in the late 15th century, inspired by designs used on tapestries and carpets that were in turn influenced by Roman and Islamic decorative art. Enclosed in a square or rectangle, clear lines of low planting weave around and into each other, resembling Celtic or geometric knots, which gives the garden feature its name. It often looks like a mini parterre (see pages 96–7),

with low, neatly cut hedges that act as frames for colorful flowering plants. Originally, a knot garden wouldn't have had such hedges, consisting instead mainly of low herbs and flowering plants in patterns much like a perennial version of bedding. So, don't feel restricted by dark green hedging, and summon up your inner Tudor gardener.

Knot gardens scream "focal point." Essentially large pictures on the ground, they open up plenty of freedom for design and planting—great for filling a courtyard, imposing order in a front garden or creating an eye-catcher anywhere. The style suits traditional properties, but with modern design and plant choices it can also complement contemporary buildings.

PLAYING WITH PATTERN

Most knot gardens are found, and work well, alongside old properties such as cottages or country manors, helping to bring them to life with highly concentrated pattern. Although the knot garden has a long tradition, its patterns can be modern, going beyond formal squares to embrace diagonal lines, zigzags, and concentric circles. The only loosely held rule is that the design should form a "knot" somewhere in the lines (above), although there's nothing to stop you breaking that rule, too.

PLANTING IN KNOTS

Knot garden hedges (above) are usually created from dark green *Buxus* (box). But it doesn't always have to be this way. Prostrate rosemary, variegated *Pittosporum* species, and *Euonymus japonicus* "Microphyllus" are all happily clipped into low hedging. Or do away with the hedging altogether (right), creating instead a pattern from low-growing perennials such as *Lavandula angustifolia* "Hidcote" and *Berberis thunbergii* f. *atropurpurea* "Atropurpurea Nana." Other plants to use include *Thymus serpyllum* in different colored cultivars, *Stachys byzantina* (lamb's ear), *Lavandula angustifolia* "Munstead," *Vinca minor*, *Chamaemelum nobile* (chamomile), and *Santolina chamaecyparissus* (cotton lavender).

Parterres

A good parterre is one of the most breathtaking garden sights. Large areas of sculpted ground, with clipped hedges and an array of colorful plants, all grown solely to produce an immaculate, huge pattern, stop people in their tracks and deliver year-round interest.

The parterre, simply meaning "on the ground," was invented in France during the Renaissance, which began in the late 15th century. Parterres consist of entire garden layouts based on elaborate patterns where planting areas are lined with clipped hedges and topiary, and filled with flowers, all separated by paths that allow you to wander around and enjoy the manicured features. Parterres are designed to be appreciated from above, such as from the upper floors of a house, where their patterns—not necessarily easy to see from ground level—are made gloriously visible.

A parterre is undeniably ostentatious, its immaculate symmetrical layouts, perfectly clipped plants and straight lines dictating formality. Ripe for reinvention with modern ideas of pattern, parterres work well in large-scale public spaces—such as contemporary museums—but just as well as a living masterpiece at home.

NEW INTERPRETATIONS

At Broughton Grange Gardens, in Oxfordshire, UK, designer Tom Stuart-Smith has breathed contemporary life into the parterre (below) by mapping out hedges in the shape of plant leaf cells as seen under a microscope. Low *Buxus* hedging (*Euonymous japonicus* "Microphyllus" is a good alternative) ripples like plant tissue, the "cell" spaces filled with relatively low bedding such as joyful spring tulips.

THE MODERN PARTERRE

Parterres now are smaller than their grandiose ancestors, due to the shrinking size of the average garden (top left) and the cost of maintaining such complex features. At the same time, ever more creativity is being shown in their patterns and design features. Some parterres consist purely of clipped hedging, while others have much larger elements, including chunky hedges for a more minimalist look.

Informal parterres exist, using quirky angles (center left) or cloud-shaped hedging with soft undulating edges. A traditional framework in a parterre can be made to look modern, too, with careful use of contemporary colors or plants, such as ornamental grasses and North American prairie flowers.

VERSATILE FORM

A parterre can have paths running through or around it. You can add water features and sculpture, or just stick to hedging. In gaps, think about using colorful seasonal plants, such as alliums, or a single block planting of more permanent *Lavandula* and *Santolina*, as seen at Ham House in Richmond, London (right).

PATIOS, PATHS, AND DECKS

Flat areas are so important in a garden. Not only are they among the largest outdoor features, but they also create a framing edge to plantings and space where you can breathe, walk, and sit. You can introduce pattern of all kinds onto the ground, using beautiful materials, from a simple grid of slabs to more elaborate curves and arcs in setts or tiles.

Slabs and paving

Stone slabs, available in natural cut stone or composite stone-effect, and in different colors and finishes, offer comforting solidity and texture. Use large slabs in a consistent size for big grid patterns, or in smaller or mixed sizes for something more intricate and striking.

A well-laid patio can last a lifetime, and it's this permanence and solidity that make paving so appealing. Paving gives you the reassurance of sure footing, in any kind of weather—and its even surface is perfect for chairs or tables.

A stone path or patio also tells people using the garden where to go, instinctively following the space it creates. If you use high-quality well-installed materials, there's nothing more striking or transformative, making gardens feel neater and building obvious areas of interest.

LAYING OUT

Usually slabs and paving will need to be laid on an impermeable concrete base for stability, where rainwater runoff can be directed to planting areas or water channels via a built-in slope. How closely you lay the slabs will increase or decrease the gap between for pointing, and this plays a key role in emphasizing or softening the pattern. The larger the pointing gap, the more marked the grid pattern will be (left). Reducing it to only a few fractions of an inch will make the grid lines more subtle (above).

SHAPES AND SIZES

Paving ranges from squares and rectangles, including particularly narrow rectangles, called planks (top), to more random shapes. Sometimes slabs come in triangles or hexagons (center right and left), or stone can be cut to a bespoke shape (left) at an extra cost.

Size and shape dictate your pattern options. The most common pattern is a grid where slabs of the same size are set next to each other square on or offset by 30–50 percent in a mix of sizes (top), or laid in zigzags for a herringbone effect.

MATERIALS AND COLORS

The color of natural stone slabs is defined by the type of stone and its source. For instance, sandstone (below right) and limestone (above right) come in a range of shades of light beige to dark brown; slate (above) is a dark gray to black with hints of purple and blue; and granite can be found in dark and light grays and a pink-beige.

Composite slabs, made from crushed stone recast into shape, offer a greater choice of color. Porcelain slabs also come in many colors and styles. They are cast into shape in the same way as indoor tiles but are tougher and able to withstand the elements. Porcelain can also easily be used inside and out, linking the home better with the garden.

Polished or cast concrete opens up options for the largest slabs. It has few joins and is perfect for minimalist design. Concrete slabs are created in situ, cast into any shape you want—useful for supersized pattern—and can be stained in any color or painted after laying.

TEXTURE AND EDGES

Natural stone slabs can be smooth (cut), textured (tumbled), or natural (riven)—illustrated top to bottom in that order. Edges too can be perfectly cut or more rugged. Cut stone looks the most modern and can have the tightest joins, while natural, rugged stone is great for a traditional look.

The more texture stone has, the more grip, which is important outdoors, especially in the rain. Before buying stone, always test its grip when wet. If the stone is intended for a shady area, choose more texture because slippery algae can build up quickly.

Bricks and pavers

Brick is a beautiful material, available in a large range of colors, softly textured and small enough to form a vast array of patterns. Using brick you can create lovely traditional paths with plants self-seeding into them, or form clean and sharp modern industrial and decorative designs.

As bricks are smaller than slabs, they lend themselves more easily to making patterns, including grids, stack bond, herringbone (below), basket weave, curves (right), and circles. The pattern will have an effect on the sensation a patio or path evokes, even creating a sense of direction. A narrow brick path winding through a lawn or meadow, for instance, with the bricks laid end-to-end, creates a stronger line than bricks placed horizontally. You can also use brick to play with perspective; running bricks from side to side makes an area look wider, while running them from top to bottom gives the appearance of a longer space.

Laying bricks on concrete, like slabs, produces an extremely solid surface with minimal long-term maintenance. They can be set onto hardcore and sand for a permeable surface that allows water to drain through.

PATTERN JOURNEY

By carefully designing the layout of paths from one area to another, the pattern runs through the garden, acting as a line of sight and directional tool telling people where to look and where to go (opposite, top). It also acts as a contrast to the plantings, the edges of the bricks and pavers helping to frame the plants (right).

SHAPES AND SIZES

Most bricks come as a standard 8½ in. (21.5 cm) long rectangle, but they are also available as smaller "clay pavers," which can look very attractive. They are also available in double length for a more linear look. If you shop around, you can find bricks in many different shapes, such as S-shape, W-shape, H-shape, axehead, squares, and hexagons—all excellent for creating a patterned surface. Or try tegula blocks (left), which are roughly the same size as a normal brick but slightly wider.

COLOR AND SHADE

Bricks are sold in a variety of colors, from gray, black, and off-white to the more traditonal rusty reds, allowing you to create different moods and effects. Mixing subtle shades in a herringbone design (below) or circular pattern (right) produces a striking but harmonious feature. As well as fired clay, bricks come in cut stone and cast concrete, the latter fading in color over time.

Choose your color carefully, as matching the brick color of a house is notoriously difficult and "close but not quite" can look jarring. If you can't find an exact match, go for a contrasting color or choose a different material, such as slabs..

ELABORATE DESIGNS

Use bricks to make a bold pattern statement, like the circular and stepped centerpiece above, or the black and white zigzags below. Pavers (right) are even more versatile and can be produced in almost any pattern. Bear in mind also the size of the area. A strong pattern across a large area will have extremely high impact, drawing attention from everything else.

Setts and cobblestones

The combination of natural solidity and the detailed patterns created by so many small blocks make setts and cobblestones a timeless garden feature. They are an elegant option, whether you live in a farmhouse, suburban semi or modern apartment.

Generally, what we think of as cobblestones are correctly called setts. The difference between the two is that cobblestones are rounded, somewhat flat stones found naturally and then laid, whereas setts are pieces of stone cut to a fairly uniform square or rectangle block.

Setts can be the size of bricks but are often smaller. Their regular, four-sided shape opens up great variety in the patterns in which they can be laid. When planning how to use setts or cobblestones, it's best to think of them of as enlarged mosaic pieces.

SETT PATTERNS

Due to their small individual pieces, setts can be laid into more detailed patterns than brick or slabs, as shown to spectacular effect in Rossio Square, Lisbon (opposite, top). Also, the greater pointing gap surface area between sett pieces accentuates those patterns. Simple patterns include grids and squares with rough-cut pieces, which work well alongside traditional houses, and smooth sawn-stone pieces, which look good next to modern buildings. More complex patterns include circles and swirls (opposite, bottom left), diamonds, stripes, zigzags, stars, and even labyrinths (below). Cobblestones (opposite, bottom right) are more versatile still, allowing you to paint abstract patterns on the ground.

CURVES AND CONTRAST

Due to the small size of setts in relation to bricks and pavers, it's far easier to design patterns that curve and to do so with neat, clean edges. In the image center left, contrasting charcoal and light gray setts create repetition patterns, while above left similar colors are used to make an abstract pattern.

MIXING COLORS

Using stone in two or more colors instantly provides more options (right). For example, you can alternate the color of a stone, creating strips of different colors or have an accent color at repeating intervals. Generally, it's better to avoid too many colors, otherwise the pattern can become a little overwhelming.

FINISH

Setts are available in a contemporary smooth sawn finish (above) as well as the traditional rough cut (right). Either finish introduces texture to a flat surface thanks to the increased number of edges. Compared to larger slabs, this creates greater visual interest and reduces slipperiness.

MATERIALS

Setts come in exactly the same materials as slabs, including sandstone, limestone, and granite (right), in tones of gray and beige. The range of tones can also include warm oranges and reds, and cool blues (below). Cobbles are found in the same choices of stone, as well as flint, but also as natural pebbles and rocks (below right).

Tiles

Since the earliest civilizations, tiles have been used to decorate walls and floors, inside the home and out. They offer by far the greatest opportunities for outdoor pattern because of the huge variety in their shape, color, and decoration.

In a way, a tiled area in a garden looks and feels like an outdoor carpet, or neat wrapping paper, coating a patio or path in a stylish and often colorful design (right and below, in Marrakesh). One of the effects of a pattern laid over a surface is that to the observer the design smooths out physical imperfections, turning an expanse of tiles into one neat patterned surface.

Traditional clay tiles are sold with a natural matt finish or a shiny ceramic surface, either hand or machine painted. Mass-produced porcelain tiles have imbedded patterns that are hard-wearing and tough. There are even tiles that can withstand heavy frosts, allowing tiled outdoor floors in colder countries.

A DESIGN FOR EVERYONE

Outdoor tiles come in all manner of sizes and colors. There are thousands of pattern options, from diamonds to checkerboard (right, on an open terrace), using uniformly colored tiles. In terms of design, simpler patterns with zigzags or squares tend to feel more modern or formal, while smaller intricate patterns offer a more traditional, homely feel. On paper, mixing tiles (above) shouldn't work, but it can turn an awkward space into a shabby chic patchwork of color. Why not start collecting old tiles you find in shops, skips, and trunk sales, ready to create your own highly personalized pattern.

STYLE AND TONE

Tile style and pattern will have a marked effect on the feel of an area. Small terracotta tiles (top left) tend to look rustic, suitable for cottages and other older properties, while clean-cut porcelain (above) looks modern, ideal for minimalist settings. Glazed tiles (above left) set in a herringbone pattern can suit most settings, from traditional to contemporary industrialist chic.

SHAPE

Tiles can be bought in a wide range of shapes, including circles and hexagons (right). You can use a mix of colors to create new effects, such as 3-D patterns (below right). We are so used to seeing squares and rectangles on patios and paths that unusually shaped tiles are a refreshing pattern statement.

PAINTED TILES

Unlike other forms of outdoor flooring, tiles have the added benefit of pattern painted onto their surface. This is done mainly by machine, although hand-painted tiles are also widely available. They come in all colors, so you can use painted tiles to match your paths and patios to other colors in the garden, such as flowers, cushions, furniture, or building materials. Repeat the same tile across an entire area or mix tiles up (left) and let your creativity run wild with color, shape, and pattern. It's a little like designing a painting, but using tiles as your paint.

Mosaic

The Romans secured the mosaic's place in design history, adorning floors, walls, and ceilings in intricate patterns made from fragments of coloured stone, glass, marble, and other materials. Mosaic is still just as exciting as a way to embellish patios and paths in detailed, colorful artwork.

Mosaic—the creation of pattern, using tiny pieces of stone, tile, or glass—has fallen slightly out of fashion, not because of the way it looks, but rather the time and expense involved. But don't let that put you off. By focusing on small areas, and even creating the patterns yourself, costs become perfectly manageable.

For some, minimalist pattern is the order of the day, with just one or two colors laid in simple designs looking elegant and enriching an outdoor space. The joy of mosaic is that the small pieces allow for wonderful levels of texture, detail, and gradual shading of color. Whether as a focal point or subtle ornamentation of a surface, mosaic is a feature that will enhance many gardens.

Not only does mosaic look beautiful, it also offers good grip thanks to its many tiny edges, so is a popular choice around swimming pools. To speed up the laying process and reduce cost, mosaic pieces are often sold joined together by mesh, although this approach limits freedom in pattern creation.

A WORK OF ART

Outdoor mosaic can act as a bridge between graffiti and art, but with a longer lifespan than any painted surface. Above right, a highly detailed and carefully created series of swirls wouldn't look out of place in an art gallery. Minimalist patterns (right and above left) turn paths into striking floor-based sculptures that contrast beautifully with surrounding plants.

CREATIVITY AND FUN

As mosaic is constructed using many little blocks of color, it suits chunky, simple images, such as the palms above. The small mosaic pieces are like the pixels on a TV screen—from a distance the image elements will blur and look clearer. Pieces can be any shape and are usually random fragments of tile or glass. Below right, equally sized rectangles are used to make a colorful curving pattern, while below left, irregular shapes and sizes have been set into a path for an abstract effect. Under water (left), a simple two-colored mosaic takes on a gently shimmering pattern that's constantly on the move.

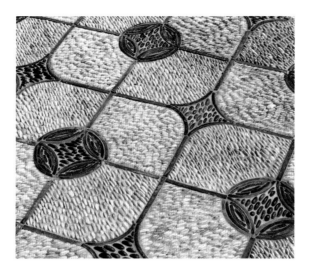

ELEGANCE

Mosaic doesn't have to be a riot of color or blocky imagery—it can be used to create beautiful pattern as a surface-enriching decoration, almost as clean in color as paint. The path below left has a simple but exquisite golden line running down the center, enhanced by subtle cream mosaic pieces laid with clean curving lines. Above left, cobbles create a sharp path design, while below, a grid pattern in soft, muted colors makes an elegant modern-looking floor. Top right, a subtle mix of shades of blues, purples, and browns creates a 3-D wavelike pattern.

Ancient gardens of Egypt

Pattern in gardens isn't a new concept. Many features we are familiar with can be traced back as far as 5,000 years to the gardens of ancient Egypt. Few temple and palace garden remains exist, but countless drawings and hieroglyphs record inspirational garden layouts, plants, and designs.

Early Egyptian gardens started, as they did in most civilizations, as a practical source of food and water. Like later Islamic and Moorish gardens (see pages 176–7), they were enclosed in walled courtyards that formed an integral part of a house.

Life in Egypt revolved around the river Nile, an essential source of water in a desert landscape, and homes and gardens were always located close to its banks. Water was carried or channeled in rills (narrow canals) to gardens, where it was stored in rectangular or T-shaped pools, usually in the center of the garden. The pools were often filled with fish and aquatic birds (above), both for ornament and food, surrounded by edible crops, such as date palms (*Phoenix dactylifera*) and figs (*Ficus carica*), which were also grown for shade against the burning sun.

It seems that the ancient Egyptians were just as advanced in horticulture as they were in construction, sculpture, and agriculture. Grapes (*Vitis vinifera*) were widely cultivated for wine and food, and other plants grown for consumption included pomegranates, avocado, olives, onions, lettuce, garlic, cucumbers, watermelons, beans, pulses, and many herbs.

Pattern in gardens emerged early on, with plants mirrored along an axis and laid out in rows around the central pool, adding to the symmetry that was so important to the Egyptians. Gradually, as with architecture, gardens became a symbol of status and wealth. Columned arcades and loggia were common, as were steps to and from leveled terraces. All these surfaces, as well as paths and walls, provided the opportunity for painted, tiled, and carved patterns. Wealthy Egyptians would decorate their gardens in stripes and more elaborate pattern, while in the grandest settings further pattern was provided by the colorful repetitive imagery found in hieroglyphic writing.

Although gardens played an important part in the layout of palaces, temples, and tombs, most now exist only in ancient Egyptian records. At the Karnak temple complex, near Luxor, however, the remains of many kitchen gardens can still be seen. Here productive gardens were laid out as well as a

botanical garden for medicinal plants. In addition to their uses as food, perfumes, and medicines, the plants also played a part in religious ceremonies, evidenced by their appearance on statues, carvings, and other stone symbols relating to powerful Egyptian gods and the pattern of the seasons.

We know many of the plants the ancient Egyptians grew and why they grew them, thanks to their records in drawings and hieroglyphic writing, as well as gifts left for the dead in burial tombs.

Various *Cyperus* species were used for making parchment, but also as decoration, alongside poppy, cornflower, hollyhocks, and waterlilies. Other popular plants included *Ricinus communis*, for caster oil, and *Juniperus* species, for medicines and as part of the embalming process. All of these are particularly sculptural plants with natural pattern to their leaves and shape, introducing to Egyptian gardens unmissable plant-based patterns that are still as popular in gardens today.

A fresco (opposite), discovered in a tomb dating from about 1350 BCE, depicts an ancient Egyptian garden, with birds, fish, and lotus flowers in a central pool, edged with papyrus plants and surrounded by date palms, sycamore fig, and other plants. Gardens like this were an integral feature of monumental building complexes such as Queen Hatshepsut's burial temple in Luxor (above).

Decking

The long, narrow planks used in decking open up all kinds of pattern possibility in gardens. Decking is incredibly malleable, too—easily cut, bent, and shaped. All this, plus wood's wonderful natural texture and look, make for fine outdoor flooring.

The usual pattern wooden planks create when laid out is a repetition of line and rectangle. But they have so much more to offer. Wood is a versatile material that can be cut and manipulated easily on-site into almost any shape and size, even bending into curves. Below, for instance, bars of wood have been set in alternating squares for a checkered pattern.

SHAPE SHIFTING

Decking edges can be cut into angular or curved shapes (right) to create a design or pattern on either side of the deck. This is much easier—and cheaper—than using stone for the same effect. There's no limit to what shape the area is because, once the underlying structure has been built, the edge can easily be cut and smoothed to any pattern.

You can also bend decking. This is usually done by cutting grooves into the back of the wood and then softening it with steam, while bending the decking into shape (below left). The specialist work and underlying structural support involved make bent decking a more expensive option.

LIGHTWEIGHT VERSATILITY

Wood is a light material compared to stone, so decking can be raised to whatever level you like. You can position it above other areas in the garden to create a viewing platform (above) or lift it to the same height as other areas, such as the level of an internal floor.

TYPES OF WOOD

Decking planks (left and above) are usually made from treated softwood like pine, with grooves cut into them for safety. But that isn't the only choice. Various hardwoods, including ipe, yellow balau, and western red cedar, make for beautiful, hard-wearing decking planks that can be left in their natural state or stained. Soft wood can be used without the grooves, too, although it won't last as long. Position decking in a sunny area and it won't form the algae that leads to slippery surfaces—although jet washing regularly will solve that problem.

STYLES AND POSITION

The combination of wood—whether left to color naturally or stained—and how the planks are set will transform a space. From top left, clockwise: a sweeping curve brings drama to a pond edge; natural planks cut into an angular edge next to a low-clipped hedge create a strongly defined shape; stained wood makes a deck look new and fresh, ideal next to modern and urban buildings; staggered planks in natural rough timber produce an authentic, jungle feel; two lengths of clean natural planks set at ninety degrees to each other make a clear area demarcation.

Gravel and resin-bonded gravel

Look at gravel closely and you see the natural pattern of its fine stone grains. But it's the broader textural qualities of gravel that can add dynamic forms to a garden, whether the stone is raked into patterns, gives shape to larger areas or offers fixed pattern in its resin-bonded form.

As a natural material, gravel looks appealing and feels pleasing to walk on. The fact it's loose and so moves around over time can be both a positive and a negative. On a sloped surface, you'll forever be raking the gravel back up, but on a flat surface with edging it will stay put—apart from when excited dogs or children send stones flying.

For walking comfort, the depth of gravel is the deciding factor—2 in. (5 cm) of decorative gravel over a 2 in. (5 cm) hardcore base is usually enough. Any more than that and feet sink too far. Driveways need a deeper sub-base to allow for the weight of vehicles.

All gravel can be laid easily into large patterned shapes; you simply need to edge the area. Gravel is wonderful as a background to pots, stones, and plants, or as a path with self-seeding annuals growing in it to soften edges. Resin-bonded gravel fixes fine gravel in place using a solid resin, opening up design options for set patterns using different colored gravels.

SHAPING GRAVEL

By marking areas of gravel with an edge, you can create many different patterns, such as circles and linear shapes (above). Gravel can also be raked into patterns, as seen in traditional Japanese gardens (left), although you don't need a Japanese-style garden to use this technique. To rake patterns into gravel it's best to use a uniformly colored stone rather than a mix.

CONTRAST

As gravel forms a uniformly textured and colored block, it contrasts perfectly with other materials, as well as complementing them, so heightening the pattern of a garden layout. You can enhance the contrast using different materials and different colors, or by pairing similar tones to create something elegant. Above, white gravel punctuated by lines of small plants blends seamlessly with a modernist home. Below, a gravel edge makes a harmonious link between a lawn and a concrete path while also accentuating their curved shapes. It's practical, too, acting simultaneously as a water trap for runoff during heavy rain.

GARDEN CANVAS

An exciting use of gravel is as a planting backdrop or canvas. Because gravel is stone, it lends a natural, authentic feel to a scene, which complements plants, often enhancing their shape and contrasting with their colors. Left, *Ophiopogon planiscapus* "Nigrescens" (black mondo grass) creates a sharp contrast with light gray gravel and pebbles, which have been planted with small succulents. Below, a buff gravel makes an attractive foil to a low topiary hedge, amplifying the pattern of the garden layout and the sculpture-like forms of the cacti.

PATTERN ON PATTERN

Plants and materials can easily be placed into a gravel area to create further pattern, such as the natural stepping stones above. Below left, gravel and low hedging sandwich areas ready to be planted with bedding or long-term planting, giving the garden a strong striped pattern. Right, a checkerboard pattern with color and texture contrasts has been created by alternating wood and gravel-filled squares.

6 WALLS, FENCES, AND STRUCTURES

Walls and fences and other vertical structures, such as steps, pergolas, and sculpture, offer fantastic opportunities to transform a garden through pattern. These upright surfaces significantly increase the potential area for design, especially in smaller gardens.

Brick walls

Today, bricks come in more shapes, sizes, and colors than ever before. On floors, they need to form a flat and stable surface, suitable for walking. On walls, though, you can play around with texture, different colors, and 3-D pattern.

For centuries, architecture has exploited patterned brickwork. But this hasn't really filtered into ordinary gardens because of the cost, with expensive pattern usually the preserve of public-facing facades. That's a shame because a garden is the space that we spend most of our time looking out onto, at home or even at work.

If you are building a new wall from brick, consider making a further feature out of it by incorporating a central patterned emblem or running a pattern across the entire surface. Even a small detail, such as a change to the pattern on some of the top or central rows, will add a unique twist to your garden.

BASIC BRICK PATTERNS

British designer Tom Massey displays a beautiful brick wall above in the traditional stretcher bond pattern (overlapping for strength), made contemporary using slimline, buff and brown bricks in a tasteful patchwork of color. You can make various slight alterations to this pattern to create different looks. Use paint to introduce color variations that still allow the pattern to show through (far left), or create new permanent patterns by laying bricks fired in different colors (left).

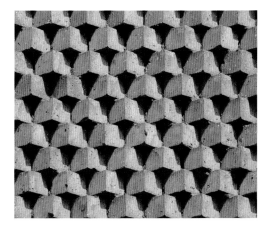

3-D PATTERN

Outer layers of brick make for some highly ornamental patterns. A sawtooth pattern (top) is created when bricks are set at an angle, which draws out both shadow and texture. For a simple but dramatic 3-D effect, set bricks in the stretch bond pattern but with some jutting out further than others (left). You can play around with any number of 3-D brick patterns, even using lighter, cheaper, and more versatile wooden blocks to produce brick-like effects (below).

TRADITIONAL PATTERN

An old wall (top left) still shows evidence of a Flemish bond, where full bricks and black half-bricks alternate in rows. Tops of walls are a great location for pattern details, such as rows of arches (above). Introducing pattern to the layout of a brick wall, such as a wave effect (left), can transform its appearance. The curves here are enhanced by another striped pattern using red bricks. Walls that aren't straight are rarely seen because of the cost of laying skills and materials, and the limitations of space. But, given the chance, they can be spectacular.

CONTEMPORARY TWISTS

You can give a wall a modernist look with some careful design choices, such as laying bricks so they jut out horizontally in a more haphazard way (left). Perfect grids always look clean and modern, especially with smooth-surfaced brick and muted colors, such as black, beige, and gray-blue (center left). For a rustic-cum-modern mash-up, try laying horizontal and vertical reclaimed bricks in earthy colors (below).

GLAZED BRICKS AND PAINT

Bricks with glazed surfaces (above) have been around since the Industrial Revolution—often seen on grand Victorian houses. They lend themselves to contemporary pattern, too, making the most of color choice and modern manufacturing techniques. Paint is a relatively low-cost way of creating a similar pattern effect (right), which can be enhanced by thick pointing gaps.

Drystone walls

We think of drystone walls as traditional rural barriers—rugged and beautiful. Today, with modern stone-cutting techniques to add to centuries of experience, this artful patterned garden feature takes on a new lease of life.

Traditional drystone walls will never be out of fashion, but modern drystone techniques offer an opportunity to reinvent a classic. Precision-cut stone is perfect for neat, layered patterns, while rougher natural stone allows you to explore shape and pattern right across a wall. Concentric circles, repeated sharp corners, changes in color—everything is possible, depending on what stone is available. Locally sourced stone is more sustainable due to low transport times; and it will unify your garden with your home area.

A LOOK FOR EVERYONE

The photos on this page show something of the sheer variety on offer from drystone walls. Clockwise from top right: regular-sized flat stones are sandwiched between natural boulders in a light-colored curved pattern; golden limestone is set in a neat pattern and planted with wall-loving weeds; a Mediterranean look is created from thin slices of slate set in a zigzag pattern; the same stone can also be used horizontally.

MODERN DRYSTONE

Clockwise from top: gabion baskets are an efficient way of building drystone walls quickly and relatively cheaply, while the mesh adds a further layer of pattern; in Lanzarote, repeating low semicircular walls shelter grapevines to create a naturally occurring pattern; cut stone, rather than natural boulders, makes for a more contemporary look; large cut rocks interspersed among smaller stones form a chunky pattern.

Tiled walls

Tiles have covered and decorated the outdoor walls of gardens in warmer climes for centuries. You won't find so many tiles in cool places, where they might crack in freezing temperatures. But that's all changing now, thanks to advanced tile manufacturing techniques.

Like designer wallpaper, but made for the outside, patterned tiles look fantastic on balconies and enclosed yards near houses, or as a focal point in large gardens. Portugal and Spain, in particular, have a wonderful range of tiled walls for all to see, with pattern after pattern lining whole streets as each building facade is adorned in different designs. Bringing this effect into gardens makes for beautiful wall features that don't have to cost the earth. With such a range of outdoor tile now available, any look is possible, from faux stone and wood through to modern patterns, as well as something more classic.

TRADITIONAL

Intricate hand-painted tiles cover the walls of Casa de Pilatos in Seville, Spain (above), linking together into many different patterns. Each tile is not only painted but also textured, as the pattern has been cast into the tiles. The use of just one single type of tile on a home in Spain (left), makes the surface of the wall feel larger, smoother and a single, unbroken entity. This contrasts well with the plain yellow wall in front.

TYPES OF PATTERNED TILES

There are endless ways to create tile patterns in gardens. In the Court of the Myrtles at the Alhambra in Spain (right), simple square tiles have been used in different colors and then arranged into a fun and vibrant pattern. At the Real Alcázar, also in Spain (below), a gated entrance is made to feel more homely with azulejo glazed tiles that have individual patterns hand painted onto them, then repeated and framed to form a larger pattern.

MOLDED TILES

Tile-based pattern doesn't only come from color; texture and molded surfaces are great, too, such as the circle and flower pattern center right. The terracotta tiles on the right have been hand decorated by children in a playful collage of patterns at the Wellington Botanic Garden, New Zealand.

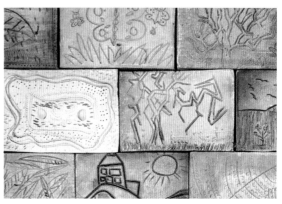

CONTEMPORARY TILES

A grid pattern of stunning gold gilt tiles (top) creates a futuristic look and an uncomplicated backdrop to golden grasses and contrasting white flowers. Large dark slate or porcelain tiles (above), hung in a vertical pattern, make a satisfying continuation between wall and floor. Slate-effect tiles arranged around an outdoor fireplace (right) in northwest USA introduce a natural edge, similar to a drystone wall.

PATTERN INFLUENCERS

Chapter one of this book discusses the importance of "pattern influencers," including color, texture, and shape. Here, the impact of influencers can be clearly seen. Wooden tiles look almost smooth in a relatively muted pattern (above left), providing a beautiful backdrop to the multitextured plants, which in turn help the minimalist container pond to stand out as the focal point. Stone-effect tiles in cream and brown (above) combine to create a modern, highly textured, natural-look wall. A bold green, blue, and white striped tile pattern (left) is set off by repeating cone-shaped wall planters.

Paint and render

Painting patterns or images onto the walls of a building or garden might seem a daunting prospect. Perhaps it will look too eccentric, and won't it be high maintenance? Don't be put off—painted walls hold massive potential for design, so take the plunge.

Let eccentricity run free and paint whatever pattern you like on your walls. Anything is possible; if it can be drawn on paper it can be scaled up for your garden. It's true that outdoor paint won't last much longer than five to ten years, so think of it as a temporary picture that can be renewed or replaced. Paint, after all, is the material that's easiest to change at a whim. Why not assign one wall to be painted in a pattern, like an outdoor picture, that you can change every year—or sooner, if you feel adventurous. Render is a longer-lasting alternative—a cement mix that can be applied in numerous colors.

BRIGHT AND BEAUTIFUL

Australian artist Reka unleashes unrestrained pattern across a building in Shoreditch, London (below), to mesmerizing effect. In the 1930s, French artist Jacques Majorelle commissioned architect Paul Sinoir to build a Cubist villa in his Marrakesh garden (bottom). Its striking blue and yellow paint scheme produces a minimalist, repetitive pattern.

NEW PERSPECTIVES

Painted patterns on walls are a fun way to play with perspective. Below, painted warped cubes make the wall look distorted. The abstract painted pattern on the right gives depth to an otherwise flat wall.

WALL ART

Pattern turns the garden at the Andaz Hotel in Amsterdam (right) into an art installation. Dutch designer Marcel Wanders uses an uncompromising black, white, and green color scheme with pattern running through the picture, floor, and topiary shapes.

In a London street (below), you might assume it's the neon colors that make the wall art stand out, but the bold clothing patterns are potentially just as attention-grabbing.

Fences

Pattern may not spring to mind when you think of fences, but timber lengths instantly become a linear pattern simply when placed together. Look to fencing as a chance to introduce a high-impact pattern across a large area of your garden.

Fences have a transformative effect on gardens, with their size and the visual weight of their vertical presence both big factors. The timber used, the way it has been cut and finished, and the pattern built into it will all change the mood of a garden.

There are many types of fence, from the familiar head-height wooden panel fences—intended to provide some privacy—to lower picket fences that mark a boundary, metal fences for extra security and lightweight fences to contain animals. Whatever the purpose you have for a fence, think carefully about the finish and pattern to make sure it's right for your space.

HORIZONTAL OR VERTICAL?

Whether fence slats are laid horizontally or vertically makes a big difference. Horizontal slats, especially when smooth and cut straight (above), make a beautiful pattern, which draws the eye along the fence and creates an easy path for climbing plants. Vertical slats look good, too, and make a fence feel higher (below), drawing the eye up to trees or views above.

FINISHES

A neutral paint or a colored stain can transform a fence into a chic style statement (above), creating a perfect contrasting backdrop to green foliage. Chunky stacked timber (right) forms a visually—and physically—heavy fence that's satisfyingly solid. Even when surrounded by furniture and climbing plants (below), glimpses of a fence can underline how patterns contribute to a garden.

WHAT IS A FENCE?

Solid upright timber posts (right) form
a linear pattern, enhanced by the
secondary pattern of their varying
heights. The posts are physically
strong but visually light, allowing
views through the gaps. A similar
approach (below) involves precision-
cut timber embedded in the ground
in a contemporary pattern that
demarcates the planting and the patio.

PATTERN STATEMENTS

A metal fence of differently sized glass panes (above) creates a pattern through shape and the color difference between the glass and metal. Shiny metal rods of equal height, and equally spaced (right), weave through a lawn to form a highly sculptural but robust fence. In St Petersburg, Russia (below), ornate cast-iron patterned fences, held between huge brick pillars, have been painted, further increasing their presence and focus. All this can be replicated on a small garden scale.

Screens and panels

Closely related to fences, screens and panels lend a garden space a sense of privacy without completely blocking out views. They are also great for screening an ugly feature, or loosely defining the edges of garden areas.

Screening can be achieved with plants or with pots, but panels and trellis are a more substantial design tool. These structures are made from wood, metal, glass, stone or concrete, usually incorporating see-through patterns that are either innately good to look at or become so once plants colonize them. Their more ornate nature can make screens and panels a costlier option than fences, so they are perhaps a best bet for use in smaller areas.

PERFORATED PATTERN

A screen can largely perform the function of a fence, but with greater scope for seeing through to the other side. The shape of stars cut into a metal screen (right) are reminiscent of Islamic design, lending an exotic touch. Large, unequally sized rectangular windows punched through weathered steel panels (below) offer glimpses of what lies beyond.

SCULPTURE TO CLIMBER

Designer Andy Sturgeon's large sculptural bronze "fins" (above) screen parts of the garden for privacy but also create intrigue. Simple trellis (left) is used for similar screening purposes, while also allowing climbing plants to take a hold and create further pattern.

BRUTALIST PATTERN

See-through concrete blocks are available in many designs, which, when stacked together, form solid patterned screens (below). Carved stone—and even blocks of glass—can also be used.

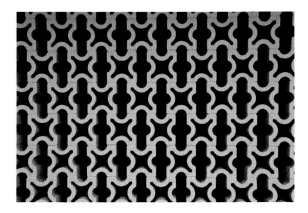

Carving, molding, and friezes

The carving or molding of pattern into stone and wood—called a frieze when it runs along a wall—is an underused feature in Western garden design. Such pattern work has a special sophistication and beauty about it—and it lasts.

Throughout Eastern and Middle Eastern palaces and temples, carved wood and stone are commonplace, inside and out. Their patterns can be purely esthetic or a vehicle for symbolism, text, and story. In gardens, their limited use of color—as many aren't painted— provides a beautiful, simple contrast or backdrop to planting and architecture. Despite the highly intricate detailing of carvings and moldings, their subdued color makes such intense pattern soft rather than overwhelming. Finely detailed patterns work particularly well alongside large-leaved plants, such as banana plants, highlighting their shape and lush green color. In the West, concrete is also cast and molded into minimalist patterns, with big, bold shapes in abstract design. Both styles are well worth consideration for use in a garden to transform a simple wall into an outdoor patterned work of art.

INTRICATE CARVING

In Putrajaya, Malaysia, a Moroccan-style pavilion (above and left) displays all the molding and carving so frequently seen across Morocco and other regions of Moorish influence. These patterns are exquisitely beautiful and tactile, with texture drawing your attention while avoiding competiton with other brighter patterns or features nearby.

MINIMALISTIC MOLDING

Clockwise from top: repeating frames in cast concrete act as a striking break between the patterned wall and living moss patterns; a cast triangular pattern with living wall segments plays on shape, light, repetition, and shadow; a corrugated effect is generated by simple rows of cast concrete cylinders divided by lines; circular patterns form ripples and islands over a grid between the segments, creating almost sculpture-like levels of texture.

Steps

With vertical risers and horizontal treads, steps merge the benefits of wall and floor. Use this combination to reach new levels of design with bespoke pattern that turns steps into sculpture.

Perhaps it's the natural pattern formed by a succession of horizontal lines that means steps are always a strong garden design feature, or simply their functionality that draws us to them. Whatever the reason, although many wouldn't look to steps as a canvas for art and pattern, when they are used in this way, the result is always arresting.

Pattern can be incorporated into steps by the type of chosen material and how it's laid, through to the shape of the actual steps and any additional pattern detail. A step's tread can carry the same pattern as the riser, flowing into one another, or be entirely different, so creating contrast and additional interest.

STYLE AND IMPACT

Two completely different examples demonstrate the exciting possibilities of pattern with steps. In the garden on the left, bricks are set in a variety of patterns, with a simple beauty. It's easy to see each step, too—a safety plus. Above, in San Francisco, 163 steps have been lovingly decorated on the risers in a tumbling mosaic pattern, visible when you are facing the steps or on the way up.

CASCADING PATTERN

Integrating lighting into steps (above) is good for safety but also exaggerates the natural linear pattern of the feature. Three flights of steps set at ninety degree angles (right), and zigzagging along a hillside, create platforms that urge you to pause as you make the transition from one stage to another.

SIZE AND FRAMING

Semicircular steps (left) fan out into a dominating pattern that allows people to walk up from all angles to reach the next garden level. Carved balustrades and urns (above) introduce ornate pattern to otherwise basic stone steps.

DOMINATING FORM AND SHAPE

Seated terraces spanning an entire outdoor amphitheater are linked by simple steps (above), which adds subtle pattern to the landform (see pages 202–5). A futuristic design (left), brings terraces and steps together to create an intriguing geometric pattern, while a gentle but visually striking wave pattern adds beguiling interest to a short flight of steps (below left). Four huge stone spheres in a symmetrical pattern (below) give greater dominance to a plain but solid set of steps in a lush tropical garden.

NATURAL PATTERN

Steps don't always have to be straight. Natural stone blocks in the garden on the left give easy access to a raised platform. Simplicity is key, with the three boulders arranged in a satisfyingly uncomplicated design. It's easy to overlook the composition as being a pattern, but the act of stacking three stones in this way creates an element of visual rhythm that draws attention.

PATTERN BOOSTERS

The wide waved edges of a large fountain (right) give patterned shape to a large-scale scene, with steps following and framing the outside. The narrowing of the fountain and steps at the top makes the feature feel longer than it really is. Form in the neatly clipped hedges below highlights the random natural pattern in the stone steps. Bright color on the edges of the decked steps below right adds a neon layer of pattern—as well as an element of safety.

Sculpture

Arguably, sculpture looks best outside among trees and plants. Surrounded by the dense detail of leaves, branches, and flowers, sculptural form stands out, its edges and shape clearly defined and elements picked out in natural light and shadow.

Sculpture—carved, cast, or molded—offers a wider variety of shape, size, and material than most other garden features. It can carry pattern as much as any other surface, whether the pattern is the sculpture itself or the cladding added to the piece for an extra dimension of interest.

No matter how big or small your garden is, or whatever its style, there will always be a sculpture to suit it. In terms of positioning, treat sculpture as a focal point, either within the garden or viewed from a window indoors. Consider repeating the pattern on the sculpture elsewhere in the garden or on nearby buildings to increase the sense of unity of space. A sculpture will also work just as well as a stand-alone feature.

PATTERNED SURFACE

A sculpture can represent anything—a human figure, an animal, a plant, or an abstract shape. Pattern can then be used to add texture and visual effect. In the garden on the right, a human form has been created by artist Joseph Hillier from sheets of metal, making patterns in shadow and layers, all encased in a further grid-like diamond pattern of wire mesh.

PATTERN EXAMPLES

A street sculpture in Marrakesh (right) has pattern added in the form of copper wire wrapped around the figure holding the sphere. Leaf patterning lends the sculpture below, by artist Jonathan Hateley, a natural appearance and a sense of movement, while helping it blend well with the surrounding shrubs and trees. In a large pond at the Tremenheere Sculpture Gardens in Cornwall, UK (below right), pattern itself becomes the sculpture, floating serenely on the water's surface.

EXPLORING SHAPE AND FORM

In Missouri, USA, orange curved glass sculptures (left) snake
out of the ground cover like exotic animals or flowers, in
recognizable rhythm. A metal sculpture (above) by the
Danish-Icelandic artist Olafur Eliasson twists and loops in
a sinuous pattern at the Serralves Foundation gardens
in Porto, Portugal. Texture-patterned stone spheres (below)
feel at one with the shapes of topiary around them.

FRAMING AND FOCUS

A cottage garden (above) is given a modern twist with a circular metal sculpture that frames the view of vivid planting and a thatched gazebo beyond. Almost hovering over a waterfall, a delicate stainless steel leaf sculpture (above right) creates a bold 3-D focal pattern. Decking has been turned into sculpture (right) by British designer Thomas Hoblyn with his inventive use of carved wood. It looks beautiful and provides a perfect counterpoint to the planting behind.

Arches and pergolas

A familiar sight in gardens around the world, arches and pergolas are elegant focal points that draw the eye. On a more practical level, they also act as a clear entrance to a garden area and create welcome shade for seating.

Arches and pergolas can be built from various materials, most commonly wood or metal, sometimes with stone and brick pillars. Depending on the material, style, and color of the structure, it can be made to look traditional or contemporary, with pattern playing its part in pushing the style further one way or the other. A pattern of straight-edged geometric arches cut out of metal can look futuristic, for example, while organic shapes in natural wood or rusted metal have a more traditional feel. Patterns added to the sides and roof then double up as ornate trellis support for climbing plants.

SIMPLE OR EXTRAVAGANT

What looks like a feature based on laburnum trees (above left) is actually a series of repeated arches of yellow orchid—though it could be recreated using many different kinds of plant. The graceful simplicity of the arch structure makes the repetition pattern stand out strongly. In Thailand's Sukhawadee House (above right), a row of ornately detailed arches are used purely for decoration, painted with pattern and capped with planting.

MATERIAL CHOICES

A wooden pergola is given a modern twist using semitransparent colored panels (top). At the Real Alcázar, Spain (left), stone walls covered in render have arches cut through them for access and to frame the view of a fountain. British designer Jo Thompson's romantic garden (above) uses patterned concrete arches floating over a water garden for enclosure and ornamentation.

PATTERNED SPACES

The trees on the right have been clipped and trained into a natural series of arches, repeating in a pattern of curves and straight edges—the primary focus and backdrop of the view. A pergola provides some geometric shade at an office block (below), using long parallel slats of narrow wood to form a highly contemporary and minimalist look, the pattern enhanced by the shadows.

METAL WORKS

The South Bank Grand Arbour in Brisbane, Australia (above), shows what can be done when contemporary style meets a big enough budget. More than ⅔ mile (1 km) long, the feature is constructed of more than 400 curling steel tendrils linked by horizontal climbing beams, allowing bright pink bougainvillea to add vibrant color to the pattern. For garden theater on a smaller scale, modern laser cutting techniques have been used to create a metal pergola (left) with an intricate roof pattern.

Patterns with pots

Although small compared to other garden features, pots can still make a big impact. And when it comes to pattern, their surfaces offer a feast of decorating opportunity.

Pots contribute to garden pattern in two ways. They have pattern as an intrinsic part of their shapes and surfaces, and you can also arrange them into a pattern. In a garden with little intentional pattern, a pot with a bold finish can really draw the eye, brighten up a dull corner and add a deliberate touch of chic. Plain pots can be grouped or arranged into patterns for added impact, and, even better, you can combine the two approaches with a group of patterned pots. Perhaps the greatest thing about pots is that, unlike most garden features, they are so easy to move around and change, allowing you to make easy pattern experiments.

BUILD YOUR OWN

You don't always have to buy your pots. The above container could be made at home, using two different colored metals cut into a cube, with a simple pattern on the outside. A neatly clipped low hedge planted in the pot adds to the layered modern design.

POT EXPERIMENTS

A simple row of small terracotta pots
with the same spiky plants (above)
creates an easy pattern. Pebble-filled
metal cages (opposite, top) manage
to produce two patterns—from the
round pebbles and the grid mesh.
Repeated spiraling tall metal containers
(opposite, center) create pattern from
the diagonal lines and varying heights.

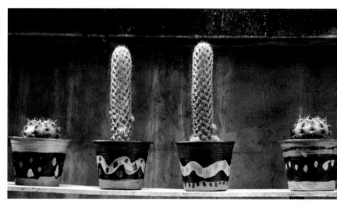

HAND PAINTED

A row of beautifully hand-painted blue
and white pots (left), filled with the same
plant species, use pattern to lead you
down—or up—a flight of steps. A simple lick
of red, white, and black paint manages to
turn a simple rectangular trough (above)
into a cubist statement piece. Four small
cacti (above center) sit in pots decorated
in fun painted patterns easily recreated
by children—or adults, come to that.

7 PATTERNS
AND WATER

Water brings a sense of calm, reflective light, and movement to a garden, as well as the soothing sound from running water and fountains. Use pattern to enhance water features through shape or by adding pattern with designer edging, a stylish base, and beautiful plants.

Ponds

A pond is a strong focal point, and a pattern related to it has a high visual impact. The play of movement, reflection, and space above the water's surface all draw the eye. And even better than that—a pond, whatever its shape, is a wildlife magnet.

If you visit the great gardens around the world, ponds feature in almost all of them. They add the kind of calming atmosphere that only still water can create.

Once practical additions to gardens in the earliest civilizations, ponds were used for storing water, bathing, raising fish to eat, and giving livestock a place to drink. Today, there are ponds that still serve such purposes, but our love of these water features has evolved to include them as decorative garden features in their own right. The most memorable ponds are those that add a pattern, making them visually compelling, stand-out features.

SURFACE ELEMENTS

At the Getty Center (left), high in the Santa Monica mountains, overlooking Los Angeles, a fairly simple round pond has been modernized with a floating maze of hedging. In garden designer Andrew Duff's show garden at the 2019 RHS Chelsea Flower Show (above), a large, sinuous bronze statue wrapped in curving pattern rises from his pond. Its reflection casts patterns across the water's surface, over which tiny metal leaves float in sequence.

POND SHAPE

Think about using the pond itself to generate pattern.
Play with the outline to create a spiral (above) or other
patterned design, or by repeating the pond's shape to make
a basic repetition pattern (right). By doing so, you'll produce
a bold statement pattern that draws attention. Technically,
you'll need to consider how a pond with a potentially
awkward shape can be lined. Cement or butyl pond liner
will help, or you may prefer to have a simply shaped pond
cavity and then create a more complex design around the
pond with materials like paving, stone, and wood (below).

BASE MATERIALS

Natural ponds tend to be murky, so not much thought is given to what lies at the bottom. When the water is clear, however, the base of a pond becomes an important opportunity for pattern. In compact situations, such as an urban courtyard, clear water over pattern creates a calming and beautiful focal point (left, above and below). Any watertight material can be used to make the base, such as stone, cement, mosaic, or patterned tiles (below). Regular cleaning will be necessary to keep the water clear and maintain the impact of the base pattern.

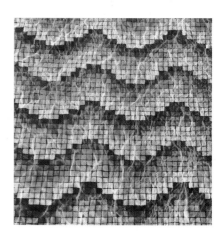

FRAMES AND EDGES

A pond edge is an opportunity to introduce framing pattern as an eye-catching alternative to pattern on the base. Adding tiles, setts, pavers, or decking (left) around a pond accentuates its shape—and also frames the water and contents of the pond like a living painting.

PLANTS

New foliage and flowers can enhance any pond. Many plants have a naturally attractive patterned structure that brings order and design to the pond. *Equisetum hyemale* (above), known as rough horsetail, and *Cyperus alternifolius*, the umbrella plant, are dramatically shaped plants that thrive in ponds, offering intriguing natural pattern. Perhaps the best known of all pond plants, waterlilies (left) spread repeated pattern across the water's surface with their floating pads and add glorious splashes of summer color with abundant multipetaled flowers.

Swimming pools

Larger than ponds, and with cleaner and clearer water, swimming pools present an ideal opportunity for patterned sides and bases, which you can then accentuate with nighttime lighting. A swimming pool's deliberately sculpted shape allows you to construct patterned layouts as far as your imagination and budget allow.

In less temperate countries, swimming pools are seen as luxuries, while in places with plenty of hot weather, they are a necessity for keeping cool and making the most of leisure time. Although natural-looking swimming "ponds" are increasingly popular, there's still a place for a traditionally designed, crisply carved out pool—and it's here that pattern can be used to awesome effect.

Unlike a pond, a swimming pool needs to be free of clutter. You can add the odd flourish, however, from statues to patterned steps and even a pool bar, if you have the space and fancy a taste of luxury.

POOL EDGE

Edging on swimming pools plays a safety role. It allows extra grip on an area that can become slippery and hazardous, as well as giving a visual cue to help define where the pool begins. Edging also provides plenty of excuse for design. Using complementary patterns, such as grids, parallel lines or curves, you can give the pool edge a distinctive frame (above and left).

PATTERN AND COLOR

The crystal clear water in a swimming pool places more importance on the materials and colors used for its base, where tiles can create any pattern you like (top left). When it comes to color, though, the entire world seems intent on keeping the base an enticing aqua blue, when it could be any color, such as a deep royal blue, a subtle shade of green or gray—or even black (left). Lighter colors, however, do let you spot anything dropped into the pool and resting on the bottom.

SHAPE

Swimming pools don't have to be rectangular. They can be pretty much any shape you want—even curly (right), although that won't be particularly useful if you want to swim lengths. That said, you can introduce a range of pattern to a pool while still keeping it functional. Whether you choose curved, zigzagged, or a more abstract shape, the key is to make sure the pattern is visible, while allowing enough space for swimming.

Fountains and falls

Running water adds movement and sound to a garden. This is particularly helpful in drowning out road and other noise in an urban environment. Fountains and falls come in many forms, from elegant arcs of spray to animated cascades of water tumbling down a series of levels or steps.

Fountains have been a feature of gardens for thousands of years—for drinking, washing, or ceremony. Now they are recognized as key focal points, bringing animation, decoration, and relaxing sound to a garden. Patterned fountains were a part of Egyptian, Roman, and Moorish life, often at the center of courtyards or as the eye-catching conclusions to loggias and walkways. This can be replicated on a smaller, simpler scale in the home garden, where patterned materials and repeated water patterns can turn fountains into liquid sculpture.

FOUNTAIN PATTERNS

Unlike other water features, such as ponds and swimming pools, fountains operate vertically as well as horizontally (above), allowing you to make striking patterns. Using water sprayed from multiple jets, you can play with arches and other shapes (left), spraying upward in a sequence of different patterns and heights that create something visually spectacular.

MATERIALS

Whatever materials you use to build a water feature, they can also express varieties of pattern. You can introduce all kinds of design through mosaic and tiles (left), and by carving or casting with cement, stone, metal, and wood to embed pattern into a feature.

SHAPE

The shape of water features that fall from multiple levels can be used to introduce a pattern into that shape. Stepped falls, for example, slow the speed of the water and increase its movement and sound (above). The steps can be angled into a simple spiral or angular pattern (right).

Patterns in Islamic gardens

Pattern and geometric symbolism have always infused Islamic gardens, forming the main focus of indoor-outdoor living spaces. These gardens are laced with religious and spiritual meaning that link the elements and nature to Allah and the idea of paradise, which together build the foundation for the use of pattern. This style, and the religious practices that underpin it, may be very different to what you see in equally patterned Japanese and Chinese gardens, but there are parallels in the deep meanings and respect for nature that they all share.

Arranged in a symmetrical quincunx pattern (below), and with further pattern within pattern on its tiles, this garden could feel chaotic, but the plain walls, limited color palette and large leaves help to unify the design.

To understand the use of pattern in Islamic gardens, it's important to remember that they are born out of necessity, being situated in harsh, hot climates with baking sun and limited water. The gardens, usually at the heart of the home, are enclosed by walls to create shade and act as an outdoor hall. Water, where available, runs through the garden, its scarcity adding to the symbolism and sense of paradise on Earth. In the past, water would primarily be used in the buildings of the rich, such as the 13th-century Generalife palace in the Spanish city of Granada.

Generally, Islamic gardens divide into formal and symmetrical patterns. The quincunx formation is common, with gardens split into four by paths or water rills and with a central fifth point in the form of a fountain or other water feature. Other gardens have rills running down the center, along its entire length, with the garden mirrored on either side.

The use of carved and tiled patterns and symbols on walls and floors is another obvious design detail of Islamic gardens. Over the centuries, techniques improved and tile art became increasingly elaborate. Designs differ greatly, from simple plain tiles set out in grids and shapes, and small tiles

Traditionally, Islamic tiles (above) were hand painted, allowing for incredible feats of elaborate wall and floor art.

Fountains and pools (left) are usually lined with colorful patterned tiles, brought to life by the shimmering surface of the water.

that form intricate colorful geometric mosaics, to extremely sophisticated carvings and hand-painted tiles.

Such complex and detailed patterning alongside plants should, theoretically, appear chaotic, but it works harmoniously, for a variety of reasons. Viewed from a distance, patterns with fine, repeating detail create a solid backdrop, which can be enhanced by the use of limited color palettes. For example, a white and blue painted tile wall viewed from a close position can be appreciated for its clear two-color pattern. Seen from the far side of

the garden, that same wall turns into a purely light blue screen as the pattern becomes more difficult to discern.

Plants in hot climes tend to be on a larger scale than their more temperate counterparts. The stately silhouettes of topiarized ornamental orange trees and the fleshy leaves of succulents and palms, for instance, contrast dramatically with patterned tiles. While flower color plays its part, green foliage dominates, allowing tiles to take on the color role that would be played by the mixed borders of cooler, wetter climates.

Rills

In nature, a rill is a narrow water channel, like a stream, cut into rock. You can create your own rill, using hard landscaping materials to produce exciting patterns that draw the eye and lead you through all areas of a garden.

A rill is one of garden design's most elegant features. Long gullies of slow-moving water create relaxing movement that draws you along their length, following them to see where the water ends. Rills are often found in Islamic gardens (see pages 176–7), used in the earliest examples to move water around for irrigation as well as for symbolic and decorative effect.

Today, we don't need rills for any real practical purpose, using them instead as focal points and to link garden areas. Show gardens by top designers regularly feature rills in all kinds of pattern, often incorporating rugged materials, such as rounded pebbles or brick. These, in turn, create their own simplistic patterns and, used as an uneven base, make the water ripple like a stream.

LAYOUT AND SHAPE

At Rousham Gardens in Oxfordshire, UK (below), a winding rill leads to a bathing pool, its wavy pattern wrapping around curves, enticing you to discover what lies beyond. A rill tends to be long and narrow, offering great scope for sculpting it into a variety of shapes. Usually, rills are one unbroken line—undeniably simple and beautiful. But there's so much more to them. Introduce multiple rills that run one alongside the other, or have a rill that splits and crisscrosses (above).

BASE MATERIALS

Because a rill contains running water, it tends to be cleaner than a pond—and certainly you'll want to keep its small channels clear of blockages. This means the base of the rill is always on show, presenting an opportunity to add pattern in the materials you use (left). Metal, stone, cement, and waterproof brick are all good choices.

PATTERNED EDGING

Enhancing a rill with edging makes it stand out (right and center right). Cobbles, tiles, metal, bricks, and layered or sculpted stone all work well as edging, allowing you to create a variety of designs. Because edging is likely to be repeated along the entire length of the rill, it's best to keep the design simple, with larger one-off detail and a limited color palette.

Bridges, walkways, and stepping stones

Few things in a garden provide as much fun as stepping stones across a pond or stream. There's also something especially enjoyable about standing on a bridge or walkway above water, looking down at what lies beneath the surface and across its smooth expanse. Add some pattern, and this becomes even more exciting.

If you are lucky enough to have a large area of water in your garden, then a bridge, walkway, or stepping stones are attention-grabbing ways to make the most of it. Their surfaces are also ripe for patterning, which will stand out strongly against the water below and produce intriguing reflections.

Because they can be positioned anywhere within a water feature, stepping stones create instant pattern. Even a bridge's structure can add pattern, with supporting legs shaped into diamonds or arches, and handrail supports—in wood, concrete, stone, or metal—repeating vertical, horizontal, diagonal, and even more elaborate shapes.

BRIDGES AND WALKWAYS

A bridge crosses water directly, while a walkway meanders above it, serving as a viewing platform or path. Both have surfaces that offer many pattern possibilities, with the platform you walk on the easiest element to enhance. A wooden bridge can have planks laid any way you like, from classic horizontal (below left) to diagonal, diamond, and zigzag. Using metal, you can create something even more complex (below). With its satisfyingly random twists and turns, a walkway can wrap around and highlight other elements in the water, such as plants and design features (opposite, bottom left).

STEPPING STONES

A line of stepping stones makes a quick and easy crossing, but adding more to produce a grid-like pattern creates even greater visual interest (center left). The stones can be made from traditional rough stone, such as granite, sandstone, and limestone, and cut into any shape, with saw-cut stone the smoothest. Uncut rocks allow for more natural patterns, the jagged random shapes creating something raw and beautiful (below). Also, stepping stones don't have to be "stones" at all. For a really modern look, metal can be molded into all kinds of form and pattern (top left).

8 PATTERNS IN GARDEN FURNITURE

Furniture can make or break a garden design. It's a natural focal point, often in a central position, and likely to be the most used garden feature. Think of furniture as practical sculpture, chosen for both comfort and design, with pattern embedded into the structure or added through fabrics.

Chairs

Nothing is more enticing than a quiet seating area in dappled summer sunlight—even better with an iced drink or chilled glass of wine. Good seating areas draw you to them, encouraging use of the garden as a place to read a book, have a chat, do some work or simply watch the world drift by. Throw pattern into the mix and your chairs will go from ordinary to extraordinary.

Seating turns a beautiful garden into one that's also practical and useful. If you have the space, create more seating areas than you think you'll need. There's something particularly pleasurable about a choice of spots, especially when you are chasing sun or shade.

There are as many types of outdoor chair as there are indoor choices—formal and upright, including dining chairs; lower, more relaxed chairs; and outdoor sofas and loungers for kicking back and unwinding. Pattern can be worked into a chair's structure, such as on the arms, seat, and back. At other times, pattern is carried across a set of chairs grouped together, such as around a table, rather than concentrating detailed pattern on an individual chair.

Make sure you prioritize comfort above all other considerations. But remember that a seat will always draw attention, making its look a factor worth investing in, especially as a way of adding pattern to your garden.

STATEMENT PIECE

Straight out of a sci-fi film or an ancient Eastern temple, a large hanging copper chair (left) shows what can be achieved when money is no object. The chair is constructed from sheets of repeating copper in a striped pattern, and its shape mirrors the patterns on the sculptures behind.

PATTERNED FRAMES

Many garden chairs have latticed frames that can be built into a more imaginative design, as shown on the left, where organic pattern resembling leaf veining catches the light. Rounded chairs with mirrored lines of supporting metal make a prominent feature singly, but repetition intensifies the pattern (center left).

CHAIRS WITH PATTERN

On the left, eight wooden dining chairs carry a simple design of a circle within a square. Repeated around a circular table they form a powerful pattern. Deck chairs (above) and outdoor beanbags easily incorporate patterns to suit all tastes and can be customized for a more personalized design.

Benches

A good bench is a place to perch, put your feet up and even lie down. It's particularly useful in making the ideal spot for a moment of rest and contemplation—perhaps to admire the view of your garden design.

Benches come in two forms—with backs and without—the one with a back being a more restful proposition for longer breaks. Benches without backs have a sleeker appearance, can be put against a wall and easily stowed away under a table. They also offer access from all angles.

Pattern is an intrinsic part of a bench's structure, just as it is with a chair, but the canvas of possibilities, provided by the extra width and surface area, is broader. This scale ensures a bench is noticeable from greater distances and makes it easier for a single piece of furniture to carry more than enough pattern, rather than relying on the repetition of several pieces arranged together. Wooden benches make for chunkier designs, while metal allows for intricate yet strong designs. For real statement solidity, try benches made from rock or concrete.

BEAUTY OF BENCHES

Cast-iron armrests (top) demonstrate just how finely detailed metal can be, while still maintaining a bench's strength. A wooden bench (above) needs a stronger frame, which allows it to include finer details within its core structure. On the left, thin metal bars are joined in graceful loops, creating a delicate but deceptively strong bench.

DIVERSE DESIGNS

Clockwise from top left: a minimalist serpentine bench commands the space with its shape and linear pattern; a built-in bench with basic horizontal lines doubles as a storage cupboard; zigzagging woodcapped gabion baskets are filled with stone for something both rustic and elegant; a traditional bench combines the virtues of both wood and metal, the latter versatile enough to carry a floral pattern.

Loungers

There's an air of glamour about a lounger, perhaps because it's a reminder of relaxing times on holiday beside the pool. A garden lounger on a warm day is a blissful extravagance, inviting you to just lie back and daydream—and perfect, too, for introducing a patterned centerpiece.

STYLISH COMFORT

An ultra-simple and sleek curved design in gray and black (above) multiplies into much more than the sum of its parts as each seat becomes an object in pattern. Even traditional wooden loungers (left) have some pattern to them, thanks to the slats that form the seat and backrest, while white woven loungers (below) display pattern that has been carefully considered as part of the structure.

Loungers are statement pieces of furniture, luxurious in size and with a long horizontal form. They are a particularly useful asset in garden design because, if carefully chosen, they can transform the entire feel of an outdoor space.

Pattern on loungers is constructed in the same way as it is on other seating, although the low and long form stretches and lengthens the design. The whole lounger can be shaped into a patterned structure, such as a singular angled block or looping outline. Or pattern can be added to the surface, influenced by the color and texture of the chosen materials.

Repetition of these prominent seats, like anything in a garden, becomes a pattern itself. Choose your loungers with this in mind.

DESIGNER SETTINGS

In the garden above, a touch of the Mediterranean suits pared-down metal loungers. On the right, although the surface material of this unusual lounger forms a striped pattern, the curving shape has its own, highly modern pattern, too. In a garden filled with pattern (below), stripes of wooden blocks in different shades are combined into sculptural loungers.

Tables

A practical garden necessity, a table generally has a simple surface, consisting of planks of wood either tightly butted against each other or with gaps between. This creates a satisfying basic linear pattern, but a table can be so much more.

Look for tables with a designer pattern to them, or devise your own and have it custom-built. Think about pattern influencers (see chapter one) and how even one or two of these, such as color and shape, can cause big visual differences.

Tables have a large flat plane that can carry intricate patterns. Remember, though, that this is a heavily used space, often filled with other items, such as plates, dishes, and books, which could clash with too much pattern. A table is rarely a stand-alone item; repetition of dining chairs will be a design companion.

CHOOSE YOUR STYLE

The look of the rest of your garden, home, and even visible interior furnishings should be considered when choosing a garden table. Colorful tiled surfaces (above) work well for Mediterranean and shabby chic looks, while the cool olive green grooves of the metal table on the left create a modern urban feel.

PATTERNED TOPS

An antique table (top) demonstrates
intricate pattern in a triple radial design
of three distinct patterns—with the
rust adding a texture and color bonus.
A combination of pale blue patterned
wicker chairs and a matching striped
table (above) uses pattern and color for
a relaxed bohemian look. Beautifully
crafted circular stripes (right) create
a pattern that would suit a more
contemporary garden.

Fabric

The fear that the weather—be it sun or rain—will damage outdoor fabrics means they aren't used nearly enough. Yet fabric is a carefree, easy addition to a garden, creating huge impact, especially when decorated with beautiful patterns.

Have a cupboard close to where you want to use fabrics to make it super-easy to whip them out and then store them away. Once you start introducing patterned fabrics to your garden or outdoor space it will be hard to stop, as they offer transformative impact with minimum effort. Experiment—and build up different looks for different occasions.

Rugs, cushions, beanbags, throws, parasols, table runners, bunting, and shades—there's no limit to where fabric can contribute. And just as you find when browsing through clothes shops, there's no end to the number of fabric pattern possibilities.

If you make your selections carefully, fabrics can also link indoor and outdoor spaces, bringing the garden much closer to your home. Using the same cushions on indoor and outdoor sofas, for instance, can be a powerful psychological link in forming a single, continuous living space.

INCREDIBLE TRANSFORMATIONS

If you look closely at the three photos on this page, and beyond the patterned fabrics, the decks are quite similar. But the spaces feel very different. Muted earth tones (top), with simple, clean, minimal patterns on the cushions and footstool, make for a chic seating area. Candy stripes (above) create a poolside vibe. Soft greens and grays, and a minimalist bench (left), produce a relaxed urban courtyard feel.

COLOR SPLASH

Bright-colored cushions (above right) inject instant garden excitement. Garden shade sails are brilliant for creating color-combination patterns (right). They are inexpensive and easy to hook to walls and fences.

SHADY SPOTS

An obvious though underused place for pattern in a garden is on the fabric of a parasol (left). Bold stripes draw attention, but there are any number of patterns and colors available, including more muted designs.

Contemporary urban gardens

rban gardens are the gardens of the future. They are the type most of us already have or work near, and are a showcase for innovative patterns. These gardens tend to be enclosed, stand-alone spaces, where any style goes.

One simple innovation, the modern bifold door, has opened the back of many urban homes to the outside world, encouraging us to merge the two into a single living space, with sofas outside and plants inside. Views out of homes and offices are now like displays of large-framed works of art, with contemporary urban gardens often an eclectic fusion of materials, colors, and pattern.

From floral to geometric, colorful to muted, boldness is the key, with strong details and confident lines and shapes. Such simplicity of form helps a pattern to contrast well with both clean minimalist surfaces and lush planting. Pattern that bridges landscaping and planting has become a defining element of modern urban style.

Fences and walls play a major role in urban gardens because they are so visible and often offer a larger surface area than the garden itself. This backdrop becomes a canvas for all kinds of designed pattern and planting, including the creation of living walls.

The ground itself is just as important a surface. Traditional paving, decking, and brick can be set into many patterns, using a wide range of modern materials, including clay pavers, hardwoods, or composite decking. Porcelain slabs and tiles work both inside and out, linking floors and walls of interior rooms to the garden.

The boundaries, trees, and buildings that fill urban areas often obscure views, making urban gardens mostly inward facing. This means a garden doesn't have to relate to the surrounding area to feel cohesive, unlike more open country gardens, in turn creating a freedom to explore less natural, patterned shapes, such as zigzag paths and angled planting.

Furniture plays a unique role in urban gardens because of its sculptural form and ability to create focal points. Accessories, such as cushions, blankets, and rugs, are another exciting way to introduce pattern, not least because they are easy to move around and replace. Add patterned cushions to garden chairs and you'll be amazed how much drama this simple action can add to a space. Don't be afraid to use many different patterns at once and embrace experiment, to bring vibrancy, balance, and the right feel to your outdoor space.

A contemporary urban workspace (left) uses bold block planting of evergreens with strong leaf pattern alongside equally bold blocks of slate gray diamond-formation slabs framed by porcelain-patterned tiles.

In Guangzhou, China (above), an office garden features large linear slabs of granite as a main pattern, which works in unison with the building's grid-pattern windows. Architectural leaf pattern from palms frames and softens the space and generates color.

9

LARGE-SCALE PATTERN

All the patterns in this book can also apply to larger landscapes. Architects and designers have long used pattern to make buildings more beautiful as well as functional, and to transform whole landscape vistas. Such large patterns become a part of the surrounding space, so when designing a garden, consider the impact they have on unity—and vice versa.

Landscape, shrubberies, and trees

If you look across a hillside, you'll see natural patterns in the way the colors and shapes of shrubs and trees are spread around. Over the centuries, designers have played with this natural template by adding their own unique twists.

Working with large landscapes is an exciting opportunity to use pattern and plants on a scale most gardens simply can't contain. In the 18th century, Charles Bridgeman, Lancelot "Capability" Brown, and William Kent were pioneers of the English landscape garden style, in which they reshaped entire vistas on large estates by reducing or enlarging hillsides, creating serpentine lakes where none existed before, and planting trees in their hundreds as if mere herbaceous perennials. They believed they were creating enhanced naturalistic views, but their idealized designs were, although works of garden art, entirely unnatural.

Despite the sheer scale of such landscape gardens, the pattern in their planting is just as relevant today to smaller garden design. Trees are repeated in pleasing combinations of form and color, lakes twist and snake in simple shapes intended to make them look larger, and landscape features, such as bridges and statues, introduce pattern into garden architecture.

MEGA PATTERN

"Capability" Brown began his design for the gardens at Sheffield Park, in Sussex, UK, around 250 years ago. Although they have since been added to, the patterns in the original planting of trees and shrubs can still be clearly seen (above), with mixed forms, sizes, and colors of huge plants repeated and then reflected in an artificial lake.

MAXIMUM IMPACT

Not only does landscape-sized pattern offer instant jaw-dropping wow factor, it also creates structure. Hillbark Open Garden (left), in Yorkshire, UK, features a complex set of patterns based around shape. The curving lawn mirrors the hillside, clipped shrubs echo shapes of larger trees in the distance, while the golden yew topiary (*Taxus baccata* Aurea Group) creates its own simple spiderlike spoke pattern. Natural landscapes are often full of dramatic pattern. In Japan's Naruko Gorge (below), the rich colors of fall trees blend in a vast and yet intricate and magical tapestry.

TRANSFORMATIVE IDEAS

The Universe Cascade (right) by landscape designer Charles Jencks, in the Scottish borders, is high in impact but still brings an elegant and light touch to a natural slope. Starting at the top, a series of steps zigzag and converge to a single point, the patterning exaggerated by the white minimalist stone set against evergreen shrubs, all reflected in the lake's surface. At the opposite end of the scale is the French Garden at Nong Nooch in Thailand (below), where the parterre form is lifted to another dimension, replacing whatever existed before with an ostentatious display of shapes, color, and repetition.

THINKING BIG

Designing with shrubs and trees
is no different to using smaller
perennials and annuals. All offer
different combinations of form and
color that add to the pattern. At the
Isabella Plantation, in Richmond Park,
Surrey, UK (above), colorful small
rhododendrons (commonly known
as azaleas) are repeated along a shady
woodland walk for some spring impact.
In the garden of the Medieval Bishops'
Palace in Lincoln, UK (right), fastigiate
hornbeam trees (*Carpinus betulus*
"Fastigiata") have been clipped and
planted in a contemporary, regimented
pattern with interconnecting paths.

Landforms

For millennia, humans have sculpted the ground, creating landform art from soil, rock, plant, and water. The beauty of landforms lies not only in their often spectacular sculptural impact but also in their draw as places for relaxation, contemplation, and imaginative planting.

Landforms exist everywhere in nature. They are the shapes, such as hills and mountains, valleys and plains, created naturally by the movements of the Earth's surface. They have also been shaped throughout history by the hands of humans to make the land easier to use, such as for settlements, to store water, for better farming yields, and to create lookouts and barriers for protection. Over time, soil and rock were also moved for religious and ceremonial reasons, which can still be seen, for example, in the form of burial mounds and symbols carved into hillsides.

All these formations have an unnatural, often patterned look to them, startling in scale and with lines that are more organized than those found in nature. Today, landform is used for esthetic as well as practical purposes, allowing the display of some of the world's most unexpected and dramatic patterns.

In your own garden, look to landforming to create a structure and shape within the existing terrain, perhaps to raise or lower planting or seating areas, or simply to create a land-based focal point that draws attention. Changing the levels of a garden requires good planning, but it needn't be a daunting exercise and is one that can have stunning results.

ART OF THE PRACTICAL

Around the world, sculpting horizontal ridges into hillsides makes agriculture possible where it otherwise wouldn't be. The terraced rows of the rice fields in Hoang Su Phi, Vietnam (below), are there for a practical reason, but they also make a beautiful, undulating pattern. At the Garden of Cosmic Speculation in Scotland (opposite, top right), the same land-sculpting technique explores mathematical pattern.

ALLEGORICAL PATTERN

At Boughton Park, in Northamptonshire, UK, British designer Kim Wilkie has created the landform *Orpheus* (above), an inverted grass pyramid, its ridges spiraling down to the water and the "underworld." In Dubai, Palm Jumeirah (opposite, bottom right), an artificial archipelago in a stylized palm tree pattern, is probably the world's largest human-made landform.

PLAYING WITH WATER

Landforms can introduce water features, such as lakes and ponds, to create their own simple patterns or become part of the larger feature. On the left, a terraced landform incorporates a patterned metal water fountain, the fountain itself pouring downward in a linear pattern. At the Scottish National Gallery of Modern Art in Edinburgh (below), a curvilinear pattern landform has ponds at its heart.

MOVING UP

For the height of landform design, look to the roofs of buildings. A section of New York City's High Line (above), a disused railway transformed into an urban "greenway," has its own pattern, enhanced by sculptural rings within the naturalistic planting. In Lisbon Square in Porto, Portugal (left), an entire shopping center has been encased in an abstract pattern landform to create a raised park, complete with trees and lawns.

Walls

Like any garden wall, a building facade can be covered in pattern, but the larger space and greater quantity of materials it demands, and the distance from which we view it, change perceptions and possibilities. The increased surface area becomes a rich canvas for supersized pattern.

Architects have always used pattern to break up vast expanses of wall—to introduce texture and design, or to turn what would otherwise be a stone block into something more gentle and beautiful. A number of more adventurous architects have turned these essential surfaces into works of art.

Pattern often begins as a structural element, such as windows or beams, the design being a by-product of a practical purpose. Structural walls can also be covered in an ornamental "skin," such as tiles or wood, to cover what's beneath in a more desirable pattern.

The impact of pattern on the wall of a building is significant due to its large area, height, and scale, influencing everything around it. If you can see a neighboring building from your garden, with a strong pattern to its walls, it becomes part of the garden, so, for the sake of unity, it should be at least considered when you think about your design.

MATERIAL CHOICES

In an urban garden (above), created by British designer Kate Gould, modern tiles work beautifully with green planting tones. The pattern, accentuated by the white rectangular tiles, makes the wall the focal point. A large block of flats in Sydney (right) uses glass and concrete in a grid pattern as the external wall materials, their rigidity softened by a layer of living walls and planters, added in a more random pattern.

NATURAL CLADDING

The outer surface of the apartment block on the left is clad in living walls from top to bottom, a planted patchwork that adds more greenery on the walls than would be possible in the building's footprint. The windows add their own precise, punctuating pattern. A small city home and garden (below) displays natural wood in a variety of patterns as its stand-out surface material. Linear paneling on the wall of the curved house is continued seamlessly into the garden fencing.

BRILLIANT TILES

Patterned tiles on an apartment block (left) in Lisbon, Portugal, make it look as if the building has been covered in wrapping paper. Unlike paint, tiles never lose their shiny vibrancy. In the north of India, the Rock Garden of Chandigarh (below) displays colorful broken tiles arranged in a giant mosaic pattern.

DESIGNER BRICKS

An exciting patterned wall (right) uses regular bricks arranged in different positions to create holes—for shadow—and 3-D texture where the bricks sit proud of the wall surface. The combination of bricks and latticed-patterned wooden doors creates a contemporary and satisfying look through imaginative use of traditional materials. Bricks have long been used as a way to add pattern to walls, sometimes even carved into further patterns.

STRIKING MINIMALISM

For the Neue Seeschanze apartments at Lochau in
Austria (above), architectural practice Baumschlager
Eberle has mixed a traditional tiling style with a bold
linear pattern of metal strips jutting out along the
base of each apartment and into the balconies. On
the right, another strong linear pattern is created by
severe thin strips of vertical wooden paneling, with
a central patterned opening for windows and light.

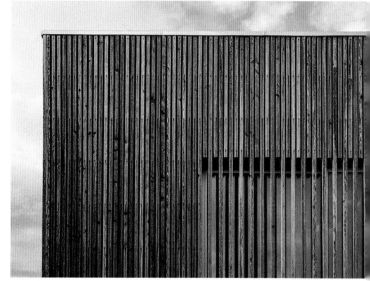

CONCRETE PATTERNS

Despite its relatively high carbon footprint, concrete
is a useful building material because it lasts well and is
malleable before it sets. Concrete can be poured into
molds to set rock solid in any pattern, such as the
stylish block pattern below, or the super-minimalist
wall bottom right, where pattern is barely visible but
exists from the window and faint molding lines.

Extreme pattern

Most of the extreme patterns designed by Charles Jencks at the Garden of Cosmic Speculation, Dumfriesshire, Scotland (below), are inspired by science and mathematics. This warped terrace explores the nature of black holes.

Join the ranks of those taking gardens to the next level with extreme pattern. Throw off the shackles of nature or accepted rules and treat your garden as a work of art, making pattern its core, worked into the very essence of the layout and incorporating other features, such as furniture and sculpture. It may seem eccentric, but if you are going to design a garden, what's stopping you from pulling out all the stops?

The 20th-century Brazilian modernist landscape architect Roberto Burle Marx took his pattern designs to the extreme, emblazoning buildings and vast city sidewalks, particularly in the urban centers of his home country. Pattern was at the heart of his designs, with planting areas, ponds, swimming pools, patios, and paths all incorporated into his abstract and trippy visions. Despite the completely unnatural look of Marx's patterns, his careful use of color and natural shapes helped those patterns to sit harmoniously in their surroundings, which in turn reflected his love of incorporating native Brazilian plant species into the majority of his designs (see opposite, top).

One of the great benefits of an extreme approach to garden design is that the space created will feel totally unique—unlike any other space in the world. When an area is completely redesigned in this way, it feels cohesive and unified because it has effectively been reinvented by the one designer, with a core pattern that holds everything together.

The extreme approach isn't all about landforms and hard landscaping—plants are vitally important, too. Some of the world's leading landscape designers today, such as the Dutch pair Petra Blaisse and Piet Oudolf (see pages 54–5) and Briton Tom Stuart-Smith (see page 96), also sculpt landscapes into patterned layout. They give a location artistic structure but with an emphasis on the plants and how they contribute to the master pattern.

The principle of transforming a landscape through structural pattern can be applied to spaces of any shape or size, including small gardens, balconies, and roof terraces (see opposite, bottom). All you need is for a pattern to dominate the whole space, not just be a component of it. You could incorporate custom seating as a pattern that continues into the rest of the garden, or take a designed floor and continue its pattern up a wall. You could also experiment with large-scale patterned 3-D sculpture and even make the layout of planting areas a clear pattern, too. Doing so will create the kind of striking and artful space that Roberto Burle Marx would have applauded.

A Brazilian tropical
garden (above) is a
dramatic statement
of Roberto Burle Marx's
free-form ideas of
bold pattern.

A pink and white London
garden (left), designed by
Ana Sanchez-Martin, is
refreshingly eccentric.
Pattern permeates every
corner of this innovative
urban space.

Windows

Always a focal point, windows attract
even more attention when they form part
of an imposing statement wall, offering a
prime opportunity for pattern. And look
beyond the rectangle—other shapes can
be nothing short of spectacular.

The importance of windows to gardens cannot be
overstated. We spend as much time gazing out of
them into gardens as we do glancing back at them
from outside—forever looked through and yet so
often overlooked.

   Patterns created from, or designed into, windows
can be highly inventive. Detailed frames with elaborate
patterned carvings or paintwork make more of the
window itself, as does the window's shape. Often the
shape of the glass and frame forms a simple pattern,
or a more intricate pattern emerges when a window
is divided into many panes. Seen together across the
face of a building, windows are ideal for creating
large-scale pattern through repetition, with pattern
influencers like color and shape having real impact.

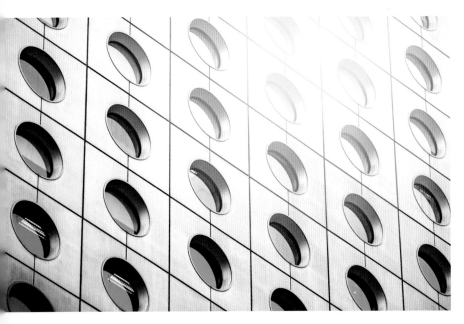

SHAPE AND COLOR

The building facades above
and left demonstrate clearly
what a difference the shape
of a window—here square and
circular—can have when repeated
en masse in a grid pattern. Color
plays its part as well, with the
cool simplicity of blues and grays
complementing and softening
harder building materials, and
multicolored windows, by contrast,
injecting some fun and vitality into
the urban scene.

PATTERN POSSIBILITIES

Just varying the width of windows over a large surface can bring that surface alive with some arresting linear pattern (left). Below, internal planters have been used in a living window pattern for a design that can be seen from the inside and the outside. Traditional windows can make just as much pattern impact, like the repeated eye-catchers at the bottom, used as a foil for a colorful painted wall and contrasting red flowers.

FOCAL POINTS

It's the windows more than anything else that become the unmissable pattern on the spectacular Casa Batlló by Antoni Gaudí in Barcelona, Spain (left). In Bavaria (bottom left), molded window frames are intricately patterned in white stucco—an energetic twist set against the rich blue walls. A standard grid of windows on a tower block in London (below) is transformed by colored panels and huge external crossed beams.

ATMOSPHERE

A courtyard (above left) at Atelier Forte in Milan, Italy, is given some garden chic by the greenery allowed to run riot around a timeless, beautifully shaped and patterned pane of glass. In India, a delicately carved window (above right) helps to create both light and shade and produces a hypnotic pattern in the shadow and sunlight. Smaller windows offer the chance for a one-off artistic feature, such as a stained-glass pattern (left).

Balconies

As populations of cities and towns around the world swell, we become ever more dependent on apartment blocks for homes, rising skyward from only a small square of land. Balconies suddenly become the most important outdoor spaces—they are the gardens of the future for many people.

Balconies play a major role in the look of our streets and are a key component of patterned facades. Like windows, they are designed in ways that together form a large pattern across often huge buildings, through repetition or more inventive pattern, such as swirls and curves. As with all designs, patterns made using balconies can be striking or subtle depending on the pattern influencers that are put into play.

Although patterns made from balconies are primarily built into the structure of the building, residents can also contribute. If you live in a drab block with balconies, why not coordinate with your neighbors to add some matching plants across all of the balconies, or even paint the walls and railings? Gardeners can add pattern into the design of their balconies, using the kind of plants, furniture, and decor shown throughout this book.

SMALL SPACE, BIG PATTERN

In Alicante, Spain (left), rounded balconies covered in a mosaic of colorful tubular tiles—pattern within pattern—have turned an apartment block from something mundane into a work of art. Around the world, an increasing number of developments incorporate substantial balcony gardens, full of lush plantings. In Milan, Italy (above), a minimalist pattern of apartment balconies has been enhanced with a lush green coat of shrubs, perennials, climbers, and small trees.

SIMPLE IMPACT

Repetition and the horizontal lines of balustrades give the block on the right a foundation pattern that has been overlaid with colored walls. These simple gestures have a huge impact on such a large scale, while still allowing for personality and personalized furniture on the individual balconies.

BALCONY AS ART

On an apartment block in Copenhagen, Denmark (above), balconies become the key pattern. They not only use shape—an elongated triangle—to draw the eye with repetition, but are also set at obscure angles for an edgy pattern that almost grows out of the building. Curved balconies (right), in Australia, replicate wave formations in a clearly recognizable nautical pattern that's intended to match the seaside setting.

Glossary

abstract a type of design that doesn't directly replicate any preexisting shapes or forms

accent plant a plant used within a group of plants to draw attention through contrast in form, texture or color

alpine a plant that originates in an alpine climate, usually at high altitude, where there are no trees

annual a plant that grows, sets seeds and dies in one year

balance when objects have the same visual weighting either side of an imagined axis

bedding a collection of plants used for a temporary display, often for one season only

biennial a plant that grows one year, then flowers, sets seeds and dies in the next

border an area of ornamental planting, adjacent to a lawn, path or other flat surface

climber a plant that cannot support its own weight and requires support from a wall or fence, or another plant, to grow upward

cobblestones naturally occurring rounded stones used for outdoor hard surfaces, such as paths

composite a material made from two or more different materials

conifer a plant that produces seeds exposed to the air (not within fruit), usually in cones, with needle or scalelike leaves and usually evergreen

courtyard garden a fully enclosed garden surrounded primarily by buildings

cultivar a plant produced by selective breeding that doesn't occur naturally in the wild

deciduous describes a plant that has adapted to lose its leaves during periods of harsh weather, such as cold winters or summer droughts

drystone wall a wall constructed without mortar

evergreen a plant that keeps its leaves all year round, even in harsh winter conditions

fastigiate plants with a very upright growth habit

focal point the prominent feature in a view, standing out more than all else

frieze a horizontal strip of carved, molded or painted pattern running along a wall, usually near the top

genus a botanical grouping of plant species that all share closely related characteristics

ground cover a layer—usually of low, spreading plants—over the top of soil

hardy capable of surviving harsh conditions, particularly those in winter

herbaceous describes a plant that doesn't develop woody stems

herringbone a pattern of brick or other material in rows of "V" shapes, like a fish skeleton

knot garden a square or rectangular area planted with low-growing plants in an interlacing pattern

landform any natural feature on the Earth's surface, which in a garden context can be applied to a reshaping of the terrain

landscape design the practice of designing and shaping an area of land, usually involving changing soil levels, shapes and plants

lenticel a visible raised pore in bark, allowing the trunk or stem to breathe

loggia a corridor or room with one side open to a garden, usually supported with beams or columns

meadow an area filled with grasses and flowers growing together, traditionally used for haymaking

minimalism a design style that aims to remove all nonessential elements or details

mixed border a collection of plants of various types, including shrubs, trees, perennials and annuals, grown together

modernism an art and design style originating in the early 20th century that rejects traditional rules

mosaic a picture or pattern made from small colorful objects, such as pieces of stone, shell or glass

naturalistic intended to resemble what occurs in nature

mortar a cement mix used for bonding materials, such as bricks together

palmate with a structure shaped like a hand, as applied to a leaf

pattern in a garden, refers to objects, plants, layout and decoration and how they relate to one another through repetition, rhythm or regularity

perennial a plant that lives and reproduces over many years

pergola a wood, brick or metal garden structure used to shade a seating area or walkway, usually with climbing plants growing up it

phyllode a large modified leaf stem that looks like a leaf and serves the same function

pinna(e) a segment of a larger divided leaf—on a fern frond, for example

proportion how one part relates to the whole

quincunx an arrangement of five objects, with four positioned in a square and the fifth in the center

Renaissance a period in Europe from the 14th to 16th centuries that saw rapid advancements in knowledge, society, technology and the arts

render a thin covering of a cement-based mix that can be applied to the surface of a wall to cover the construction materials

rill a long, narrow and shallow channel of water

scale the measurement of things in relation to one another

sett a small, roughly square or rectangular piece of stone used as a surface for patios, paths and drives

shrub a plant that usually has multiple woody stems and is smaller than a tree

specimen a plant grown as an immaculate example of its species

standard a plant trained into a lollipop shape with a clear stem free of branches

topiary any plant trained and clipped into a particular shape

trellis a structure, usually made of wood or metal—and either added to a wall or freestanding—that allows climbing plants to grow up it

unity when all elements within the garden or an area visually combine and work well together

variegation when leaves or petals have different colors or tones on their surface

Plant hardiness charts

Each plant can thrive only at certain temperatures, which is determined by its "hardiness"—the ability to survive outside in winter. To help gardeners determine which plants will be suited to their geographical location, the UK's Royal Horticultural Society (RHS) and the United States Department of Agriculture (USDA) have each produced hardiness guides.

RHS HARDINESS RATINGS

The RHS gives a series of hardiness ratings, between H1 and H7, each specifying a range of temperatures. These are the absolute minimum winter temperatures a plant with that rating can survive.

USDA HARDINESS ZONES

The USDA hardiness guidelines are presented as a series of "zones," from 1 to 13. Each zone specifies a range of temperatures, which, unlike the RHS system, indicate the long-term average annual extreme minimum temperatures at which a plant within that zone can survive.

Rating	Temperature range (°C)	Temperature range (°F)
H1a	>15	>59
H1b	10 to 15	50 to 59
H1c	5 to 10	41 to 50
H2	1 to 5	34 to 41
H3	-5 to 1	23 to 34
H4	-10 to -5	14 to 23
H5	-15 to -10	5 to 14
H6	-20 to -15	-4 to 5
H7	< -20	< -4

Zone	Temperature range (°F)	Temperature range (°C)
1	-60 to -50	-51.1 to -45.6
2	-50 to -40	-45.6 to -40
3	-40 to -30	-40 to -34.4
4	-30 to -20	-34.4 to -28.9
5	-20 to -10	-28.9 to -23.3
6	-10 to 0	-23.3 to -17.8
7	0 to 10	-17.8 to -12.2
8	10 to 20	-12.2 to -6.7
9	20 to 30	-6.7 to -1.1
10	30 to 40	-1.1 to 4.4
11	40 to 50	4.4 to 10
12	50 to 60	10 to 15.6
13	60 to 70	15.6 to 21.1

Index

Page numbers in *italic* refer to captions.

Acknowledgments

t=top l=left r=right b=bottom c=center

Cover images: main image Alamy Stock Photo/Arcaid Images; **top left to right** GAP Photos/Jo Whitworth: Designer Diarmuid Gavin; Alamy Stock Photo/paul weston; GAP Photos/Design Cube 1994; GAP Photos/John Glover: Design Karen Maskell; GAP Photos/Anna Omiotek-Tott: Designer Fiona Cadwallader. **Back cover: top left to right** ShutterStockphoto.inc/Pumidol; ShutterStockphoto.inc/sergua; GAP Photos/Paul Debois; GAP Photos/Howard Rice; Jack Wallington; **bottom left to right** ShutterStockphoto.inc/Yatra; GAP Photos/Heather Edwards: Design Sim Flemons and John Warland; Alamy Stock Photo/Sally Weigand.

Alamy Stock Photo 6 b Debu55y; 7 tr Christian Lathom-Sharp; bl David Litschel; 8 Derek Croucher; 9 cl John Keates; cr Tim Gainey; 11 c Marco Arduino; bl Marek Stepan; 13 r Mark Hamilton; 19 cr Mark Hamilton; 21 c Robert Smith; 23 t DeGe Photo; 25 b Arcaid Images; 35 t Natural Garden Images; 39 bl Steffen Hauser/ botanikfoto; 42 t Plantography; br PhotoStock-Israel; 43 tl Bloom Pictures; 44 c John Richmond; 45 bl Davo Blair; br Avalon/hotoshot License; 46 t Christina Bollen; 48 c Arcaid Images; 56 b Arcaid Images; 57 br Chris Hellier; 61 b RM Floral; 64 t Emele Photography; 74 Kathy deWitt; 78 robertharding; 79 bl Dennis Frates; 79 br mike jarman; 83 t Tim Gainey; 94 Bob Gibbons; 97 c gardenpics; b The National Trust Photolibrary; 101 cr A Garden; b Littleny; 103 br John Gollop; 104 t paul weston; b Elizabeth Whiting & Associates; 105 t Gary K Smith; b Jit Lim; 107 t paul weston; 112 t Lena Kuhnt; 113 t Matthew Corrigan; 117 tr f8grapher; 120 World History Archive; 124 tl Arcaid Images; 126 t Andreas von Einsiedel; 128 t Alamy Stock Photo; 131 l Hervé Lenain; 132 r Tim Gainey; 133 b Derek Harris; 134 tl Colin Walton; tr Sergey Mikheev; b Tony Watson; 136 br Paul Felix Photography; 138 t Digital-Fotofusion Gallery; 139 b jiGGoTravel; 141 tl Ian Thwaites; 145 c Pollen Photos; 146 b Andrea Jones Images; 148 t Hervé Lenain; 149 t A Garden; 150 t Paul Strawson; 152 l Yuval Helfman; r Sally Weigand; br q77photo; 160 r Smiling in Thailand; 164 c Kathy deWitt; 165 t Evan Sklar; 166 l Ian Shaw; 175 t Ian Shaw; 176 Art Kowalsky; 177 t Frederick Wood Interiors; 178 b Julia Waitring; 182 r David Burton; 183 l Johner Images; c Pollen Photos; 184 Pollen Photos; 185 r MediaWorldImages; b Anna Stowe; 186 tr Arcaid Images; 188 c Dennis Gross; 191 t David Burton; br colinspics; 192 br Johner Images; 193 t A Garden; 198 Phil Spinks; 200 t gardenpics; b MediaWorldImages; 201 t Arcaid Images; b Steffie Shields; 203 t Alex Arnold; b Delphotos; 204 t gardenpics; b John Peter Photography; 205 b kpzfoto; 209 t Johann Hinrichs; 210 gardenpics; 213 b sebnem koken; 214 br Edmund Sumner-VIEW; 215 tr Efrain Padro; 215 b Glenn Aguilar.

GAP Photos 2 Jerry Harpur: Design Steve Martino; 15 t Jonathan Buckley: Design Tom Stuart-Smith; b Marcus Harpur: Andy Sturgeon Design; 16 b Heather Edwards: Design Ula Maria; 17 t Richard Bloom: The Winter Garden, The Bressingham Gardens, Norfolk. Designed by Adrian Bloom; 19 cl Nicola Stocken: Designer Marcus Barnett, Sponsor The Telegraph; br Heather Edwards; Design Sim Flemons and John Warland; 20 John Glover; 21 tl Jacqui Hurst: Designer Alexandra Noble Design; tr Richard Bloom: Garden Designer Craig Reynolds; b Richard Bloom; 24 Brent Wilson; 25 c Nicola Stocken; 26 Jenny Lilly; 27 t Annie Green-Armytage: Design Joe Swift/ Sponsor Homebase; b J S Sira: Designer Max Harriman; 28 l Joanna Kossak: Designer Helene De Witte; b Clive Nichols: Garden The Great House, Burford, Oxfordshire; 29 tl Jerry Harpur: Design Steve Martino; tr Modeste Herwig: Garden Design Groen ID, Gemma Diks; c Jerry Harpur: Design Isabelle C Greene; b GAP Photos: Design Chris Beardshaw; 35 b Tim Gainey; 36 tl Jonathan Buckley; tr Lynn Keddie; b Matt Anker; 37 tl Mark Bolton; bl GAP Photos; 38 tr Neil Holmes; 40 br Jenny Lilly; 41 br Clive Nichols; 44 b Jo Whitworth; 50 t Pernilla Bergdahl; 51 t J S Sira; 52 Caroline Mardon: Garden Design by Karen Rogers; 53 tl Joanna Kossak: Designer Andy Sturgeon, Sponsor The Telegraph; tr Nicola Stocken; b Richard Bloom: Garden Designer Ryan Prange; 56 t Rob Whitworth: Design Piet Oudolf; 57 bl Howard Rice; 58 b John Glover; 59 tr Rob Whitworth: Designers Harry and David Rich, Sponsor Cloudy Bay and Bord na Móna; 60 Abigail Rex; 61 t John Glover; 64 b John Glover; 65 b Rob Whitworth; 66 b Nicola Browne: Design Ross Palmer; 67 b Abigail Rex: Garden Arundel Castle, Sussex. Head Gardener Martin Duncan; 68 t Fiona McLeod; b Dianna Jazwinski; 69 tl Elke Borkowski; tr Richard Bloom: The Swimming Pond Company, Garden designed by Paul Mercer; b David Dixon; 71 r Dianna Jazwinski: Design Adrian Hallam, Chris Arrowsmith, and Nigel Dunnett; bl Andrea Jones; 72 t Jerry Harpur: Design James Fraser; b Anna Omiotek-Tott: Designer Ula Maria; 73 b Jerry Harpur: Design Steve Martino for Arid Zone Trees; 75 Charles Hawes; 76 Jo Whitworth; 77 b Jonathan Buckley: Design Christopher Lloyd; 79 t Marcus Harpur; 80 b Visions; 81 t Christa Brand: Weihenstephan Gardens; c Jenny Lilly: Garden Jardim Municipal, Funchal; b Christa Brand: Weihenstephan Gardens; 82 t John Glover: Design Alan Gardener; 83 b Leigh Clapp: Location Spurfold; 85 b Abigail Rex; 86 t Jo Whitworth: Designer Diarmuid Gavin; 87 bl Charles Hawes; 88 J S Sira: RBC Blue Water Roof Garden, Design Professor Nigel Dunnett, Sponsor Royal Bank of Canada; 89 tl Elke Borkowski; tr Fiona Lea; b Marcus Harpur: Designer Sean Murray, Sponsor Royal Horticultural Society; 90 t Rob Whitworth: Design Barry Mayled; 91 t J S Sira: Design Tony Woods; b Robert Mabic: Designer Jeni Cairns with Sophie Antonelli; 92 Rob Whitworth; 93 Clive Nichols: Waterperry Gardens, Oxfordshire; 95 t John Glove; b John Glove; 96 Clive Nichols: Credit Broughton Grange, Oxfordshire; 97 t Nicola Stocken; 100 l Nicola Stocken; r Design Cube 1994; 101 t Jerry Harpur: Design Roberto Silva; 102 tl Clive Nichols: Designer Charlotte Rowe; tr Juliette Wade: Credit Roger Gladwell Landscapes; 103 t Design Cube 1994; 106 tr Liz Every; 107 br Lynn Keddie: Design Cleve West; 109 br Andrea Jones; 111 tl Paul Debois; 114 tr Roy Hunt: Designer Kate Gould; 115 l Rob Whitworth: Designer Kati Crome; 116 Highgrove; 117 l Jerry Harpur: Design Made Wijaya and Priti Paul; br Elke Borkowski; 122 t Lee Avison: Garden Design Angie Barker, Garden Design For all Seasons; b Jerry Harpur: Design Sam Martin; 123 t Matt Anker; bl Mark Bolton: Design Jamie Durie; 129 br John Glover: Design Karen Maskell; 132 t GAP Photos: Design Tom Massey; 136 c Anna Omiotek-Tott: Designer Fiona Cadwallader; 139 l Rob Whitworth; 140 t Marcus Harpur: Designer Sara Jane Rothwell and Joanna Roig; 143 br Annie Green-Armytage; 144 t GAP Photos; br Anna Omiotek-Tott: Designer Andy Clayden, Dr Ross Cameron; 145 t Paul Debois; b Nicola Stocken; 149 c Elke Borkowski; 151 t Joanna Kossak: Designer Martin Lines; 154 c Jerry Harpur: Location Alnwick Castle, Northumberland; 158 b Clive Nichols: David Harber Sundials; 159 tl Nicola Stocken: Designer Roger Platts; tr Jo Whitworth: Design Xanthe White; b Elke Borkowski: Design Thomas Hoblyn; 163 b Brent Wilson; 164 l Clive Nichols: Location Ridler's garden, Swansea; 165 br Brent Wilson; 169 t Stephen Studd: Designed by Christopher Tessier (Jardin de Tessier); 169 b Rob Whitworth: Design Roger Platts; 170 bl Mark Bolton: Design Kerrie John; 171 r Jerry Pavia; 172 t Matteo Carassale: Garden designed by Marco Battaggia. www.formaterra.it; 173 c Nicola Browne: Design Kristof Swinnen; 174 b Mark Bolton; 175 br Jerry Pavia; 178 t Elke Borkowski: Design Thomas Hoblyn; 179 t J S Sira: Designer Jeni Cairns, Sponsors WWT; r Victoria Firmston; 179 b Carole Drake; 181 t Ian Thwaites; 181 c Rob Whitworth: Design David Cubero and James Wong; bl Fiona Lea; 185 t Nicola Stocken; 186 c Jonathan Buckley: Design Rani Lall; b Lee Avison; 188 t Brian North: Designer John Nash www.johnnashassociates.co.uk; 189 t Graham Strong; c Hanneke Reijbroek: Design Darren Saines; b Mark Bolton; 192 bl Clive Nichols: Designer Charlotte Rowe, London; 199 t Sarah Cuttle; 202 b Charles Hawes; 206 t Stephen Studd: Designer Kate Gould; 207 b Brent Wilson; 211 t Jerry Harpur: Design Roberto Burle Marx/Gilberto Strunk; b Clive Nichols: Designer Ana Sanchez-Martin of Germinate Design; 215 tl Matteo Carassale: Design Duilio Forte.

Getty Images
147 tr Mark Turner; 162 b RapidEye; 163 t Brent Randall.

ShutterStockphoto.inc 1 jeep2499; 5 t Serge Skiba; 7 tl Redchanka; cl Yatra; br Piotr Krzeslak; 9 tl marchello74; tr buteo; 11 tl Pigprox; tr Moomusician; cl Georgios Tsichlis; cr hbpictures; br Jose Ignacio Soto; 12 r photolike; 18 t BBA Photography; 22 t photolike; b Yolanta; 23 b Phaendin; 25 t 2M media; 30 l Sabine Hortebusch; 31 c Yulia Plekhanova; r bells7; 32 tl Cheng Wei; tr simona pavan; 33 c Michael de Nysschen; 34 tl COULANGES; bl Peter Turner Photography; 37 c KCX13; r LensTravel; 38 tl Monika Pa; br ANGHI; 39 tl Sabine Hortebusch; br chanchai plongern; 40 tl COULANGES; tr Del Boy; bl Andrew Fletcher; bc COULANGES; 42 l Kathryn Roach; c Nancy J. Ondra; bl Gerry Burrows; 43 tr Gerry Burrows; bl bells7; 43 br Kazakov Maksim; 44 t ahmydaria; 45 tl abriela Beres; tr Peter Turner Photography; 46 cl Anastacia Petrova; cr InfoFlowersPlants; b Manfred Ruckszio; 47 t jeep2499; cl Yulia Plekhanova; cl Molly NZ; 49 c KajzrPhotography; r randy andy; 50 b randy andy; 54 t Alexander Prokopenko; b MandriaPix; 59 b KajzrPhotography; 62 l Evannovostro; c Charlotte Bleijenberg; r Del Boy; 63 l Gordon J A Dixon; c elliebean042; r patpitchaya; 64 l patpitchaya; 65 t elliebean042; 66 t Del Boy; 70 Felipe_Sanchez; 80 tl Oppdowngalon; 83 c Peter Turner Photography; 84 starman963; 85 t Gordon J A Dixon; c Kris Hollingsworth; 86 b Charlotte Bleijenberg; 87 c wjarek; br wjarek; 90 b Evannovostro; 98 l Kanitnon Keemkhunthod; c Vladimir Trynkalo; r lazyllama; 99 l Jen Petrie; c Jeanie333; r Elena Larina; 101 cl Ibenk_88; 106 tl mykhailo pavlenko; 107 bl Elena Larina; 108 Timof; 109 t RossHelen; bl Granadeiro; 110 t Chiyacat; c Tupungato; bl Kizel Cotiw-an; br RosKon; 111 tr Skrypnykov Dmytro; c sergua; bl In Art; br andy0man; 112 b Balate Dorin; 114 tl Elena Dijour; c Ron Zmiri; cb Lamuka; b Vladimir Trynkalo; 115 t Peyker; r Adil Armaya; 118 t lazyllama; c Ilkin Guliyev; bl fotomika; br SARIN KUNTHONG; 119 tl Bora Baser; tr A_Lesik; bl Jen Petrie; br Jodie Johnson; 121 Bist; 123 br Jamie Hooper; 124 tr kzww; b Nikolai Diadechkin; 125 t Jeanie333; cl Lester Balajadia; cr Ksw Photographer; cb Kanitnon Keemkhunthod; b Petrut Romeo Paul; 126 b Thye-Wee Gn; 127 t Photographee.eu; b aimful; 128 b aimful; 129 t aimful; bl Marco Richter; 130 l TigerStock's; c Pack-Shot; r giordano ravazzini; 131 c Dee Browning; r Andrew Fletcher; 132 l Anna Fevraleva; b Nopparat Promtha; 133 t aquatarkus; c Qzian; 135 t JoeyPhoto; cl Vincent Square Design; cr JoeyPhoto; bl JoeyPhoto; br RAYphotographer; 136 t Andrew Fletcher; bl TigerStock's; 137 t JGA; c Ralf Liebhold; bl song-A-ji; br robert_s; 138 b Garana; 139 t wolffpower; c sasiko kaan; 140 bl ADUL BUAPHAN; br Artazum; 141 tr STOCK_KO; b Matej Kastelic; 142 t Ron Ellis; b posztos; 143 tl Jon Chica; tr Evannovostro; bl Ron Ellis; 144 bl VMStock; 146 t giordano ravazzini; 147 tl Suti Stock Photo; b Marina Zezelina; 148 b HildaWeges Photography; 149 bl Joe White; 150 b szefei; 151 cl FrameAngel; cr FreshPaint; b HowdyB; 152 tl Alexander Sobol; tr llaszlo; bl Eddie Jordan Photos; 154 t Dee Browning; c PowerUp; bl 4Max; br Ranjana Perera; 155 t Jamie Hooper; bl Drew Fitzgibbon; br Bitzra; 158 tl chettarin; 160 l Pumidol; 161 t Del Boy; bl monysasu; 162 t Serg64; 164 t Ekkachai; 164-5 b PHATCHARADA DUEANDAO; 165 c lakkana savaksuriyawong; 166 c verdell galeana; r Olena Serzhanova; 167 c Martin Castrogiovanni; 168 b Appreciate; 169 c verdell galeana; 170 t Olena Serzhanova; br Ceri Breeze; 171 t Julia700702; 173 t Studio 37; b Pakhnyushchy; 174 t Tatiana Ganapolskaya; 175 bl Martin Castrogiovanni; 177 b enciktepstudio; 180 l OrangeNoire3; 181 br Theodore Scott; 182 l Sofia Sophie; c Silvie Vondrejcova; 183 r Franck Boston; 185 c July Prokopiv; 186 t Martin M303; 187 tl Franck Boston; 186 bl ariadna de raadt; br Martin Prague; 188 b Dmitrii Iarusov; 190 t Sofia Sophie; 191 bl Watchares Hansawek; 192 t Photographee.eu; 193 c Lorimer Images; b Silvie Vondrejcova; 194 Bill45; 195 Sunshine boy; 196 l Sam's Studio; c hans engbers; r kudla; 197 l MarleenS; c byvalet; r Steven Bostock; 199 b yspbqh14; 202 t Sam's Studio; 205 t hans engbers; 206 b byvalet, 207 t MarleenS, 208 tl studio f22 ricardo rocha; tr AnilD; b kudla; 209 c Cyrsiam; bl Noom_December; br alexandre zveiger; 212-13 t ThirdUnit; 212 c EvgeniiAnd; b YIUCHEUNG; 213 c ESstock; 214 t Valentina Photo; bl PlusONE; 216 l Phil Friar; r ANTONIO TRUZZI; 217 t serkan mutan; bl Jordi C; br Steven Bostock.

The RHS Images Collection 32 b Leigh Hunt; 33 b Carol Sheppard.

Christopher Lyon Anderson 156 *Digital Rendition*, 2013, stainless steel, by Joseph Hillier, josephhillier.com, The Sculpture Park, Surrey; 157 t; 157 br *Elemental*, 2017 *Pond Series* by Ian Penna.

Jack Wallington 7 cr; 9 b Garden Museum, London; 12 l; 12 c; 13 l; 13 c; 14; 16 t; 17 bl; 18; 30 c; 30 r; 31 l; 33 t; 34 br; 35 c; 38 bl; 39 tr; 40 tc; 41 tl; 41 t; 41 tr; 41 bl; 47 b; 48 l; 48 r; 49 l; 51 b Scampston Hall; 58 t; 59 tl; 67 t; 71 tl; 73 t; 77 t; 77 c; 80 tr; 82 b; 87 t; 161 br; 167 l Atzaró, Ibiza; 167 r; 168 t; 171 b Atzaró, Ibiza; 172 b Atzaró, Ibiza; 180 r; 190 b.

Steve Poole 157 bl *Releasing* by Jonathan Hateley, RHS Wisley.

Fogdog 17 br; 102 b; 103 bl; 113 b; 149 br; 158 tr John Andrews.

Wiki 34 tr Steve Law.

We have tried our best to identify everyone. If we have missed you, please get in touch so we can update future editions.

Thank you to everyone at UniPress Books, the Royal Horticultural Society, and Thames & Hudson who worked so tirelessly to create *The Gardener's Book of Patterns*. Nigel Browning, thank you for making this book, John Andrews for your guidance and fine crafting of the text, Nick Clark and Jane McKenna for the beautiful design. Thanks to Alix Wilkinson for his insightful book *The Garden in Ancient Egypt* (Rubicon Press). To all the gardeners, designers, architects, landscapers, artists, and photographers whose work is featured, thank you for the inspiration. And to Christopher Lyon Anderson, thank you for all your support on my design journey.

This book is dedicated to everyone who enjoys life's hidden layers.